Applied Literacy
in the Middle Grades

Introducing Children
to Authentic Inquiry

Lawrence G. Erickson

Southern Illinois University–Carbondale

Boston   New York   San Francisco
Mexico City   Montreal   Toronto   London   Madrid   Munich   Paris
Hong Kong   Singapore   Tokyo   Cape Town   Sydney

Series Editor: *Aurora Martínez-Ramos*
Editorial Assistant: *Beth Slater*
Senior Marketing Manager: *Elizabeth Fogarty*
Cover designer: *hannusdesign.com*
Production Coordinator: *Pat Torelli Publishing Services*
Editorial-Production Service: *Chestnut Hill Enterprises, Inc.*
Electronic Composition: *Omegatype Typography, Inc.*

For related titles and support materials, visit our on-line catalog at www.ablongman.com.

Between the time Web site information is gathered and then published, it is not unusual for some sites to have closed. Also, the transcription of URLs can result in unintended typographical errors. The publisher would appreciate notification where these occur so that they may be corrected in subsequent editions.

Library of Congress Cataloging-in-Publication Data

Erickson, Lawrence G.
    Applied literacy in the middle grades : introducing children to authentic inquiry / Lawrence G. Erickson.
        p.   cm.
    Includes bibliographical references and index.
    ISBN 0-205-36112-9
    1. Language arts (Middle school)   2. Inquiry (Theory of knowledge)   3. Interdisciplinary approach in education.   I. Title.

LB1631 .E68 2003
428'.0071'2—dc21

                                                                    2002033251

Printed in the United States of America

10   9   8   7   6   5   4   3   2   1   06   05   04   03   02

This one is for Kristen Grimmer and Michael Wright.
You make a difference every day.

Contents

Appendices

Preface

The Book

The primary intent of *Applied Literacy in the Middle Grades* is to describe how teachers in the middle grades show children how to use their literacy skills to do authentic inquiry. To accomplish this I present classroom examples of inquiry activities that illustrate how teachers help children raise questions, seek information from primary and secondary sources, and produce new texts. My goal is to show how literacy success in the early grades is sustained in the middle grades when teachers organize authentic inquiry activities that tap the natural curiosity of children. The primary audiences for this book are teachers, library media specialists, and others who teach children in grades five through eight.

To demonstrate what I mean by applied literacy, the book features real and constructed vignettes, actual classroom inquiry projects, primary and secondary sources, and detailed teaching strategies. All of this material is included to illustrate teachers showing children how their reading, writing, speaking, and listening are interesting, important, useful, and satisfying.

Chapter 1 is a foundation chapter in which I define *applied literacy* and argue for including it in the middle grades curriculum. The chapter describes how teachers combine powerful teaching ideas to show children how to use and apply their literacy skills to inquire about the world, and I introduce the idea that, with teacher direction, middle-grade children can begin to use their novice literacy skills to do authentic inquiry. In Chapter 2, applied literacy is discussed in the larger school and community context. The intent is to show how authentic inquiry is a key component of a balanced school curriculum. The chapter illustrates applied literacy with a detailed look at the classroom context that is controlled by the teacher who implements a thematic unit. In Chapter 3, a seven-step plan serves as a road map for teachers who plan to explore inquiry teaching. Chapter 4 describes how authentic literacy activities motivate and engage students, and illustrates how teachers relate inquiry and authentic literacy lessons to local and state learning outcomes. This chapter also shows how teachers must deal with two of their authentic concerns: the need to motivate and engage their students, and the need to be accountable and show how students use their literacy skills for learning. In Chapter 5, I discuss how authentic literacy activities lead to new views of school time and school space, expanded roles for library media specialists and parents, and new school and workplace connections. In Chapter 6, I provide comprehensive material on information and expanded information sources. The intent in this chapter is to show how applied literacy activities lead to a new view of information sources that goes far beyond typical school texts. Chapter 7 extends the discussion on sources of information and describes how teachers help novice learners think critically about information. The chapter features lessons on evaluating primary and secondary sources as well as illustrated examples of lessons for teaching children to evaluate Web sites. Because children in the middle grades are novices at learning from texts and other sources, Chapter 8 features mini-lessons on vocabulary, comprehension, and writing strategies. During authentic inquiry children encounter problems so teachers provide scaffolded activities to help them apply their reading, writing, speaking, and listening skills to answer questions and share new information. Chapters 9 and 10 describe applied literacy examples from Colorado and Illinois. In Chapter 9, a Colorado elementary language arts thematic unit and an Illinois eighth-grade language arts unit are featured. In Chapter 10, an Illinois middle school soil science project is described in detail and illustrates how an entire science curriculum is delivered by the inquiry method. Both examples provide a close look at what is required to successfully engage children in authentic inquiry.

The Audiences

Audiences for this text include preservice and in-service classroom teachers, reading and language arts specialists, library and media specialists, and others who teach children in grades five through eight. I've included a wide range of examples to illustrate how teachers provide detailed formats and rubrics to assist young researchers as they move from fluency in reading and writing to using their literacy to learn. The book documents many excellent ideas I found teachers using when children are engaged in authentic inquiry. The scope and detail of the examples is intended to provide readers with a selection of activities that match the wide range of children's skills and interests that middle-grade teachers encounter.

As children progress in school their interests and skills change and there are big differences across the middle grades. Middle-grade children begin making a transition from learning to read fluently to learning with texts, so that early attempts at inquiry are marked with plenty of teacher support. At grade five there is plenty of teacher guidance and, as children gain skills, the topics, tactics, and inquiry practices change until, by grade eight, they are capable of conducting fairly sophisticated inquiry activities. In order to introduce children to authentic inquiry, grade five and six teachers use easy-to-understand sources, simple information-gathering ideas, and straightforward reporting formats, ideas that are very useful when they are adapted for older children. Later, as children become more sophisticated researchers in grades seven and eight, applied literacy lessons feature more mature topics, more independent inquiry, and more technically supported reporting formats. However, at all middle-grade levels the acquisition of authentic inquiry skills requires plenty of modeling, direct teaching, and guidance from teachers.

The fact that middle-grade children are high on interests and questions and low on inquiry literacy tools makes grades five to eight a prime time for them to see how literacy works both in and out of school. All of the scenarios and teaching examples I have included in the text are from teachers in grades five through eight.

Acknowledgments

First and foremost I acknowledge the many middle-grade teachers and students who graciously shared their ideas, materials, and products with me. Their classroom stories are the heart of this text and I am eternally grateful.

I also thank the publisher of excellent nonfiction text, Grolier, for asking me to present workshops on how teachers use nonfiction to engage children. Their early support initiated this project and led me to meet many outstanding teachers across the United States who are engaging children with authentic inquiry.

For technical support with this manuscript I am most thankful for Karen Stotlar, Barbara Reaves, and David Blandford in the College of Education and Human Services at Southern Illinois University. I could not have included all the teaching materials without their expert word-processing help. Southern Illinois University also provided a sabbatical leave that enabled me to visit schools and classrooms and write.

My appreciation also goes to the following reviewers for their helpful comments on the manuscript: Diane Greene, Mississippi State University; Marian Matthews, Eastern New Mexico University; and Sara Tyler, Tarleton State University.

I am indebted to my wife, Joan, whose honest appraisal and editing of the initial drafts of the main chapters are especially appreciated. I have no doubt that her constant support during the years this book was under construction is a main reason it was completed.

Finally, I am grateful for the continued support and thoughtful comments from my Allyn and Bacon editors, Arnis Burvikovs and Aurora Martínez. They accepted my proposal, arranged for reviews of the chapters, and helped me make revisions that significantly improved this project.

1

What Is Applied Literacy?

I have always imagined that Paradise will be a kind of library.

Jorge Luis Borges

I had to stifle the urge to call out "amen" when the 1998 American Reading Forum keynote speaker, James Paul Gee, questioned whether there is a crisis in beginning reading in the United States. I was pleased when he cited sources I was familiar with. The data from a 1992 study comparing reading achievement among nine-year-olds in eighteen western nations showed U.S. students scoring among the highest levels, second only to students in Finland (Elley, 1992, pp. 97–98). And when he said a problem we should be dealing with is the drop in scores and attitudes around fourth grade, I did mutter aloud, "Right on!" Gee had put his finger on the very problem I have passionately researched in the last few years, which is the subject of this book. If there is a reading crisis in the United States, it is not learning to read, it is reading to learn (Gee, 1999).

This book describes how middle-grade teachers implement applied literacy lessons. Based on the children's enthusiastic engagement, as well as the products they produce, I believe applied literacy is a way to sustain early reading success. It may help prevent the widespread decline in reading achievement and attitudes that begins to show up in the middle grades in the United States. Of course, just as there is no single reason for what is called the "fourth-grade slump," there is no single solution. However, there is a growing body of evidence that the teaching ideas described in the following pages can be considered part of the answer to the decline in achievement and attitude that signal something is amiss.

I composed the following two vignettes to help define what I mean by *applied literacy*. When teachers use applied literacy activities, they conduct scaffolded lessons that enable novice researchers to gather, analyze, organize, and use information to answer questions and resolve concerns that the teachers and students have raised. In these vignettes, teachers arrange authentic social situations where students read, write, speak, and listen to answer questions that the students deem important. The teachers understand that real reading, like speaking, "always and only occurs within specific genres in the service of specific purposes or content" (Gee, 1999, p. 3). Likewise, when students engage in applied literacy activities they read, write, speak, and listen to satisfy an immediate and authentic purpose.

Vignette One

Sixth graders Mary, Karen, and Brian are researching famous scientists, using several different nonfiction sources. One book (Turvey, 1994) has a time line of significant discoveries that only include two women out of seventy-five scientists. Other books (Stille, 1995; Vare & Ptacek, 1993) detail the contributions of fifty plus women. Due to the discrepancy, the students decide to fix the time line and insert the women's contributions in the first book. As the students read about the contributions they repeatedly read stories of the obstacles women encounter as scientists. They write a report on how women are not accepted at science schools, not hired as scientists, or how their work is overlooked and discredited. They report, for example, that Crick and Watson received the Nobel prize in 1962 for discovering the DNA molecule without mentioning their use of Rosalind Franklin's 1952 basic electron microphotographic work. Franklin died of cancer in 1958 and was not alive to establish the connection between her early work and the DNA discovery.

Vignette Two

Two fifth-grade teachers, Margo and Jean, along with the librarian, Jack, have organized a thematic study of Native Americans for their students. Instead of only using the single chapter on Native Americans in the social studies text, they have collected over thirty nonfiction books and have found several Web sites with information for this project. They have also contacted several parents who are Native Americans, and they have agreed to be resources for the students.

The teachers and the librarian combine their class time for social studies and history with their reading and language arts time so that their students will learn reading, writing, speaking, and listening skills as they gather information and learn about Native American cultures.

The teachers and the librarian have met and agreed that, instead of the usual plan of having each student do research on one group of Native Americans, they will arrange the project so that small groups of students will study a few features of several different groups. Mario, Jamal, and Rachel are comparing the food and shelter of two Native American groups, the Inuit and the Navaho. The teachers show the students how to collect and arrange the information. The students are to use at least three different texts and one Web site in their search. The teachers help the students organize their notes and write paragraphs explaining how the Inuit had to use portable tents and ice shelters as they traveled to fish and hunt. They contrast this with the Navaho, who had permanent homes where they stayed to farm corn. The teachers help the students edit reports, make illustrated posters, and practice giving oral reports. To end the thematic study, the class gives presentations to the other students and parents. The teachers and the students are pleased with their reports and the parents were impressed because the children could easily explain why there are differences between Inuit and Navaho food and shelter.

Literacy for the Real World

As a "school watcher" I get excited when teachers connect with their students. This book celebrates and honors the fact that a growing number of middle-grade teachers have combined a host of powerful teaching practices to provide applied literacy experiences for their students. The lessons described in this book involve the practical application and use of reading, writing, speaking, and listening that enable novice researchers to acquire the skills, beliefs, and attitudes that mark specific social settings. To do this teachers organized lessons involving:

- reference skills, including searching, locating, and selecting information;
- thinking skills such as judging, summarizing, combining, and synthesizing;
- speaking, listening, and writing performances;
- informed, logical, and compelling discourse that had some useful social purpose.

The Politics of Classical and Applied Literacy

The applied literacy activities I describe in this book have a slightly different political purpose than the classical literacy activities that dominate schools. All literacy activities are political—there are no neutral literacy experiences. For example, when all the students read the same chapter or story and answer questions posed by the teacher and the text authors, the political message for the students is clearly one of compliance. Students are expected to participate, learn, remember, and perform as individuals. In the classical literacy lesson the text, the questions, and the tasks are assigned and students are evaluated by the teacher. The widely used Accelerated Reading program promotes a politic that requires a literal comprehension evaluation for every book that is read. Do not consider all of this as either good or bad; it has merit for plenty of reasons. But having to take a test after reading each book is a political situation that favors the teachers and the texts. The testing, scoring, and record keeping clearly send the message that the teacher is in control and the text and test scores have educational and social value.

On the other hand, the politics of the applied literacy activities described in this book are slightly different. For example, with plenty of teacher support and direction, students study a broad theme, select a question or concern related to that theme, decide which sources and which information to use and not use, construct their own text, communicate what they have constructed, and evaluate their own performance with reading, writing, speaking, and listening rubrics. All of this goes beyond the politic of compliance and individual test performance toward a politic of collective participation, involvement, and ownership. However, even if you think authentic inquiry has value, it has its share of weaknesses. Any political and social situation that shifts control of topics, texts, and tests away from teachers toward student-centered topics, sources, and evaluations is suspect and deserves inspection.

In a monograph titled *Democratic Schools* (Apple & Beane, 1995) middle-school teacher, Barbara Brodhagan, said that she shifted the "power" away from herself to joint student–teacher curriculum planning, and after two years she cannot imagine, "not involving the learners, no matter their age, in planning their education and running 'our' classroom" (p. 98). She went on to tell that, while students were able and willing to plan and design their own education, some students were uncomfortable and said it was too difficult. Likewise, the power shift was difficult for teachers because there was confusion about when they should be disseminators of information, facilitators of learning, or learners like the students. She said,

> Student-teacher planning of the curriculum was a messy process. There wasn't a neat curriculum guide or textbook to turn to for lessons. Identifying the significant concepts that would tie a theme together took a lot of time, but without this identification, a theme could become a series of "sound bites" that did little to satisfy students' need to learn. And there were many times when teachers had to scramble to find appropriate materials and resources (p. 99).

The approach to literacy in this book describes this messy process and fully acknowledges the shift in classroom politics that is both relished and feared. But I make no apologies for insisting that, unless schools make room for more applied literacy activities around third grade and continue to use them for at least ten years, the leveling off and decline in literacy learning will continue. The reality is that both teacher-directed and student-centered applied literacy activities are needed. Applied literacy activities that integrate fiction and nonfiction sources and content area studies with reading and language arts are not new. However, open access to worldwide information, increased use of multiple sources of nonfiction material, the use of small cooperative learning groups that compare and contrast features of one or more topics, as well as the productive and practiced sharing of reports to a community beyond the classroom signal a move toward an apprenticeship model of teaching and learning.

Apprenticeships: Learning from the Inside

One of the assumptions in this book is that each person develops multiple social literacies from living in a variety of social settings (see Bean, Bean, & Bean, 1999). Whatever literacies we acquire they are the result of spending time with other people who happen to value and practice the discourse literacy that comes with whatever territory or social setting we find ourselves in (Gee, 1996). There are home and family literacies, neighborhood literacies, and school and workplace literacies. These different literacies are not taught directly; they are acquired in social settings that are much like apprenticeships. That is, instead of reading and answering questions *about* Native Americans from texts already constructed by someone else, the students in the second vignette practiced a school-based information literacy from the *inside* by constructing their own text with information they found with help from other students and the teacher.

Gee's (1996) law school discourse example is appropriate here. He says students acquire a law school literacy not because they are directly taught *about* judicial literacy behaviors. Instead, law students are immersed in a social situation where speaking, listening, and, to a lesser extent, reading and writing are *used within* the law setting and students learn *inside* the procedures rather than explicitly about them.

Of course, some students do not take on the discourse of law school. Gee contends they fail because they chose to not become like the others in that social situation, not because they were not taught how to read legal text, write briefs, or argue legally. Gee defends this failure by pointing out that, given the fact that literacies and discourses are stacked decks that favor certain people over others, "no one should feel like a loser" (1996, p. 137) when he or she fails to acquire a specific literacy. Student failure is an especially crucial point to teachers because all students do not come equally equipped to acquire the listening, reading, writing, and test-taking literacies that schools offer. Certainly, not all literacies are going to be learned equally well by all learners.

All we can do is put forth our best effort like Jeff, a middle-school writing teacher who immerses his students in writing. He does not believe in the oft heard argument that, with over one hundred students, he cannot have them do a lot of writing because there's not enough time to read and identify all of the problems novice writers have. Instead of less writing and more teacher intervention, Jeff does just the opposite. He does not edit everything and mark all of the errors his students make. Instead, he focuses on a specific punctuation convention or sentence structure, makes his marks and comments, and, when he gets student papers back as soon as possible, he teaches about what he commented on. His students know what he is looking for at any one time so they are cued to what he has to tell them. Because he follows the rule of more writing and less teacher intervention, his students' portfolios will have thirty or more pieces of writing along with at least six formally evaluated pieces of writing in a semester. Jeff says one of the best things he notices is that, when students write more, they find other things to fix without his direct intervention. The result is that he is able to immerse his students in an apprenticeship situation where they write a lot, and they get to practice and practice. He knows from years of experience that he sees more improvement when students write more with limited but focused feedback than when students write less and are subjected to heavy amounts of teacher editing. Jeff's teaching is an example of the powerful notion that, when we are immersed in the discourse practices of any group, the opportunity to learn *inside* the procedures is more powerful than overt lessons *about* the procedures that come from outside. I believe the vignettes and Jeff's more writing and less intervention idea are close to what Gee (1996) was talking about when he wrote:

> Teaching that leads to *acquisition* means to apprentice students in a master–apprenticeship relationship in a Discourse wherein the teacher scaffolds the students' growing abilities to say, do, value, believe, and so forth, within that Discourse, through demonstrating her mastery and supporting theirs even when it barely exists (that is, making it look as if they can do what they really cannot do) (p. 145).

A Nonfiction Focus

In this book I describe what some teachers do with the Internet, secondary sources like content and nonfiction text, and primary sources like interviews, to give their novice readers a taste of the politics of real-world literacy behaviors from the inside. While the psychology of reading is not much different for literate children and adults, I consider the politics of reading to be much different. Adults are not tested when they return their books to the library. They choose what they read; they seek information that satisfies a current need. For example, I have enjoyed reading about new information on the human brain, and, recently, I have alternated between reading easy fiction, interesting historical biographies, and harder books on neurology and psychology. I was not forced to read any of the books nor was I tested and given points for reading. Instead, my interests lead me to pursue topics, authors, or genres. As I reflected on this I couldn't help but compare the politics of my reading with the politics of classroom reading. This concern is what led me to investigate the use of problem-based learning and inquiry-oriented activities in the middle grades.

When I began looking at the expanded use of nonfiction text in schools, I found that publishers were producing excellent nonfiction offerings. With the backing of one publisher I began making presentations at reading meetings across the United States about how teachers use nonfiction in their classrooms. At these presentations teachers said they were looking for ways to improve reading comprehension skills and the reading attitudes of their students. Others who attended the presentations shared what they were doing. When we combined what I was reporting with what the teachers and librarians were doing, the notion of authentic inquiry apprenticeships emerged as a powerful literacy strategy.

The teachers and librarians agreed that inquiry activities with nonfiction are a way to prepare students for life-long literacy success in a world where as much as 90 percent of their reading will involve the critical reading of nonfiction. The teachers also agreed that, while the increased use of nonfiction was a positive change, it was not easy because fiction dominates school literacy lessons.

Boutique Literacy

In 1995, at the Alabama State reading conference in Birmingham, I was near the end of my session when the audience of teachers and librarians said that, in contrast to the "gingerbread" sessions at the conference, this presentation on using nonfiction was loaded with "meat." There was a discussion about the power of fiction to engage children and the obvious bias of using more fiction than nonfiction for literacy lessons. The librarians pointed out that many children in the middle grades check out nonfiction and seek information from primary sources. There were nods of agreement when one teacher said that most of the sessions at reading conferences she's attended feature fiction plus arts and crafts or "boutique literacy" ideas. We talked about this and there was consensus that boutique literacy is popular and powerful but that, around the third and fourth grades, children are eager for the "meat" of nonfiction and ready for some inquiry-based learning.

All of this does not mean that fiction-based lessons are bad and nonfiction inquiry lessons are good. Literacy lessons that use a single high-quality narrative text and teacher-led activities on vocabulary development, fluency, and comprehension should and will continue to be used in the middle grades. The discussion at the Alabama conference only means that teachers and librarians recognize that fiction, or narrative text, dominates literacy lessons. However, they also recognize the value of introducing children to more nonfiction and expository text in the middle grades. One way of doing this is with applied literacy lessons.

Reasons For and Against Applied Literacy

In this book *applied literacy* means lessons that include a number of features. While these features are not new by themselves, applied literacy lessons include all of these to qualify as authentic inquiry.

- Teachers and students jointly plan literacy activities around interesting themes, topics, and questions. This is not a new idea but it is a key feature because successful and satisfying inquiry is based on the concerns and questions the children, with teacher help, raise about the theme or topic.

• Children use multiple expository and narrative and secondary and primary sources to gather, evaluate, and organize information that applies to their topics, concerns, and questions. This is also not a new idea. It is another key feature because successful inquiry involves searching for valid information from relevant and reliable sources.

• Children produce new texts and use the text to communicate what they learned to an authentic audience. This is also not a new idea, but it is the essential feature of applied literacy. Instead of finding answers to concerns and questions imposed from outside, children are using their literacy skills to produce a product that contains information about a question or topic they are curious about.

Recently, I was sharing this definition of applied literacy when one teacher said, "I like the concept, but I have to play it safe today. I have to stick with lots of fiction and use an occasional nonfiction article." No one can fault this teacher. Classroom teaching has always been marked by high uncertainty and change is always risky. The risks appear higher today given the relentless cry for accountability with fixed standards and high-stakes testing. So it is understandable that teachers and principals may be cautious and wary about implementing applied literacy lessons. But there are powerful educational, work, and personal reasons for doing so.

Education and Work Reasons

Despite the risks, there are several reasons for using more informational text and inquiry-oriented learning activities. First, if we think about it we know that becoming highly skilled at anything takes time—a long time. To go from learning to read to fluency to reading to learn from different text takes at least ten years. Early success in learning to read must be sustained well beyond the third and fourth grades with plenty of social situations where the task is to use reading (and speaking, writing, listening) to learn. Second, in the middle grades, as children refine and expand their literacy repertoire, they have to rely on more and more reading and writing for learning for specific purposes and special content. Very often the same directed teaching method used with fiction is used with content textbooks. That is, everyone reads the same text and responds to the same questions. While this may work for fiction that follows a predictable story pattern of setting, characters, and a plot, it does not work as well with content textbooks in which information is presented in an array of formats and concepts and ideas are organized by time frames or cause-and-effect structures. It takes a good deal of drive and desire, as well as repeated practice with timely guidance, to learn how to understand complex writing. The truth is that the teaching method that works for helping students enjoy and comprehend narrative text does not automatically lead students to comprehend social studies and science material (Manzo &

Manzo, 1995). Third, information packaging and future work settings are rapidly changing. Students successful at understanding stories with pictures and text have to deal with new kinds of text pages (on paper and on computer monitors) that mix words, images, and numbers. Instead of reading and learning as single individuals they also have to read, write, speak, and listen in highly collaborative work settings as adults. In 1999 the International Reading Association (IRA) referred to these changes in their position statement on adolescent literacy. Moore and colleagues (1999) pointed out how early reading success in the first four or five years of school does not automatically result in full literacy development in succeeding years. The IRA recognized that middle-grade literacy programs have been overlooked and urged schools to deal directly with the help adolescents need to make the transition from beginning reading to adult reading.

Personal Information-Based Passions

While the education and adult work arguments for applied literacy activities are appealing I have found that they are not as potent as the response teachers get when students display critical thinking. When students decide to redo a published time line because they have evidence that significant contributions by women scientists were omitted, or when students write a new biography that wisely combines information from conflicting published sources, teachers are sold on the practice. Teachers report that, when they use applied literacy activities, students are engaged, they read more, and they use their full thinking abilities to locate, evaluate, and use information to answer their own questions and concerns.

In addition to published research that concept- or information-based literacy leads to high engagement among students (Guthrie & Wigfield, 1997), I can add a recent specific instance when students responded positively. In 1999, Sheryl, an experienced middle-school social studies and language arts teacher in a small rural Illinois school, devoted ninety minutes for three days each week for six weeks to a comparison of the Revolutionary and Civil Wars. She helped her seventh- and eighth-grade students to integrate reading, writing, speaking, and listening with the content of American history. Jared and Clint were able to read, write, think, and report about the differences in battles and weapons in the two wars. Likewise, when Laura and Beth compared the role of women in the two wars they found that, while women played more of a supporting role in the earlier Revolutionary War, women dressed like men and fought in the Civil War. The combination of time, content, and the opportunity to use all of the language arts processes allowed students' questions and concerns to drive the learning process. Sheryl asked me to be in her classroom when the students presented their oral reports, using posters to illustrate what they had learned. It was obvious that, although they were novices, they had been authentically engaged in their search for information on their topics. Sheryl had them write short essays about the project and the following representative statements express their excitement about and satisfaction with the work they did.

> This was really different because we usually get a book at the first of the year and our teacher tells us about it. After she is done telling us about it we get an assignment. But this time we worked for a month and it was well worth it.

> I had to do a lot of things like searching on the computer and using encyclopedias. I think we should have this every year. I learned a lot like communicating with others. This was creative because we usually use one book to answer questions. I really did like doing the speeches.

> I liked this because I learned some things I did not know before about the part women had in the wars. I think we should do this in the future because I learn more. We should leave the speeches out. I don't like talking in front of everyone.

> We should do this more often because you learn more and it is more fun than using our Social Studies book.

> First of all we got partners and picked two questions. My partner was Nancy. I picked the question, Who were the generals? I picked four Civil War generals and was going to do the same with the Revolutionary generals, but I was running out of time so I only picked two. I told about their family life, childhood, what they did before the war, and how they got started in the war (if I could find it). It took us awhile, but in a way I thought it was worthwhile. I learn more this way than I do the other way.

> I think it would be wise to study this way because you just might be surprised at what you can find. If you let your mind explore you could find a lot about war and history so yes I think it's good to have creative thinking.

The comments reveal that, not only were Sheryl's students engaged by this approach, but they clearly identified the differences between learning as an outside observer who is told by the teacher, and a learner who figures it out from the inside by constructing new text. For example, the first comment describes what learning is like from an outside view—when we learn *about* something. The fifth comment, in which the student decided to limit her study to two generals in each war, describes what happens when we learn from *inside,* when we exercise control over the goal and the processes. All of the comments reflect a degree of pride in what happened when, with their teacher's help, they had most of the control of the questions and the searching, as well as the written and oral products. Of course, as novice learners students do not get to the "inside" without help from teachers like Sheryl, who tell, model, and give lots of help from the "outside."

Multiple and Individual Literacies

We all come to school with our "mother tongue" or primary language acquired in our early years from family and community. Growing up in northern Michigan, I acquired the speaking and listening literacies of my family and my hometown. When I went to school, I gradually *acquired* some school literacies so that, as an adult, I harbor a love for reading and discussing fiction and nonfiction books. But I've also *acquired* a specific content literacy—a passion for reading and writing about teachers and teaching. So my primary acquired literacy is school discourse, which allows me to be accepted as a professor of education. I have also *learned* several secondary discourses or personal informational literacies. For example, as I write this a 1960 recording of *Back to the Tracks,* by Harold "Tina" Brooks, an obscure but extraordinary jazz saxophone player who died young, is playing in the background. I don't play an instrument so I'm not musically literate. But, during forty plus years of listening to hard bop and west coast jazz recordings, attending live jazz sessions, reading jazz biographies, searching for good jazz recordings, and conversing with other jazz lovers, I've acquired some jazz literacy, a taste and appreciation for improvised music. This special informational literacy reflects my personal passion for improvised music and I've become a reasonably informed listener who can listen, talk, read, and write about jazz with others.

One difference between my *learned* discourse in jazz and my *acquired* reading professor discourse is that I *learned* the former from outside as an observer–listener while I *acquired* the latter from inside. I belong to the professor group because I acquired the language, values, and beliefs by performing alongside and with other professors. I am an "outsider" to the jazz musician set because I never performed jazz, I've only listened to it. But, although my membership is limited to the club of listeners, I value it quite highly. Indeed, all of my literacies are closely aligned with who I am and I use them as I live my life. All of my literacies, my primary mother tongue, my professor literacies, and my acquired secondary literacies define who I am.

Novice Expertise

The point of all this personal stuff is that the middle grades are a crucial setting in which we start to come to grips with who we are and who we will be. Applied literacy activities that give students choices about topics, questions, sources, and uses of information are potentially powerful avenues for developing a variety of useful literacies. Knowing, understanding, and being able to talk and write about a particular concept or phenomenon is a basic ingredient of being accepted by others. When the information we have gives us some social value with others who are important to us—our peers, parents, teachers, and others—it serves as an important component of feelings of self-worth.

One of my young adult friends provides a good example of this. From middle school through college she collected information and wrote school papers on eugenics—the science of controlling the breeding of humans to improve the species and reduce social problems. As we might expect, her beginning papers were typically simple and somewhat one-sided. Over the years, however, her knowledge base expanded along with her judgments and literacy skills. She saved her notes and papers on floppy discs and, as her knowledge base grew, she asked new questions, found new information, revised earlier papers, and applied her novice expertise to issues she encountered in high school and undergraduate college classes in sociology, history, science, and literature. Her personal interest in eugenics led her to become a relatively young content expert in eugenics. Her expertise on this topic, as well as her research, writing, and speaking skills, were a ticket to membership in the fellowship of successful students. I have no doubt that her ten-year association with eugenics information is a significant reason she was a successful student. The information literacy skills she started developing as a novice researcher contributed to her success as a student and contributed to her becoming a skilled and tenured elementary teacher today.

What would happen if schools recognized special literacies and gave students credit for developing secondary discourses? School standards specify a host of culturally sanctioned discourses that students are to learn for promotion and graduation. What if school standards asked students to become an information "expert" on a self-choosen topic? I realize that this notion has pitfalls. What is meant by *expert* and what information topics are culturally acceptable? Schools and teachers would surely be criticized for sanctioning students' informational expertise on controversial topics.

My own take on this is that local school standards could require students to demonstrate information expertise on a self-selected topic. But it is absolutely necessary to consider the local community and limit topics to what is culturally acceptable and appropriate for middle-grade students. Deciding which secondary discourses schools and teachers should either sanction or censor is a socially sticky issue. Indeed, this aspect of secondary discourse literacies reminds me how literacy is a deeply political power issue.

How Much Applied Literacy?

When I talk about applied literacy with teachers, one question that always comes up is how much class time should be devoted to the themes, research, writing, and reporting? My response is that I suppose, under certain conditions, a school could adopt this model and use it exclusively. However, given the nature of the schools as I know them, I think it is best to use the brushfire method. Like any change in a school curriculum, I suggest that teachers begin with a small-scale tryout. If it works, expand it until you are satisfied and can demonstrate that students are engaged and you are meeting the educational standards for the district and the particular school situation. Public school teaching is not a private enterprise so there is always a larger power or political presence. Some teachers tell me they feel safe using applied literacy projects for roughly one fourth of the time. They move back and forth from single text and separate subject teaching to integrated lessons and applied literacy activities. Other teachers use applied literacy activities on a wholesale level.

The bottom line is to use good judgment and consider the context in which you teach. What expectations are there in the school and the community? I suspect that, if you are like most teachers I know, you can do this if you believe it has merit. I tell teachers that a good way to proceed is to find another teacher, and for sure a librarian, select a theme and go ahead on a trial basis, say three times a week for about a month. If you are not sure about getting permission from above go ahead anyway and ask for forgiveness later.

Applied literacy activities and the use of more nonfiction represents a relatively new and potentially productive direction for the middle-grade curriculum. However, it is not meant to replace school literacy lessons that favor an artistic view and teachers and children are comfortable reading, writing, speaking, and listening to narrative texts. And school content lessons favor a separate text for different content subjects. I acknowledge the power of fiction and its rightful place in the literacy curriculum. I also advocate the use of content literacy strategies to help students learn from content texts. However, I present some evidence in this book that teachers are combining reading and language arts with the content curriculum. They are using more nonfiction and are conducting applied literacy lessons. The issue is not one of which is best—fiction or nonfiction, integrated thematic studies or separate texts? Nor does one need to tear down fiction and separate texts in order to give nonfiction and integrated studies the nod. This type of argumentative dualism is not, and never will be, productive. Instead, we need to look at what teachers are doing as they wisely introduce children to a growing body of excellent nonfiction and primary sources of information. Indeed, the one argument for applied literacy that stands out more than any is what wonderful things the children do when wise teachers use both fiction and nonfiction and give their students applied literacy experiences in an adult-like reading and writing political climate.

Teachers Combine Powerful Teaching Ideas

Implementing applied literacy activities can involve a significant change for both teachers and students. To shift from a teacher- and text-centered classroom to a student and multiple-text format involves changing a whole range of practices and expectancies. The following list summarizes, in a general sense, what teachers and librarians do to arrange applied literacy lessons. Depending on your local school and classroom situation, some of these activities will be easier to accomplish and others will be difficult to arrange.

- *More nonfiction and other information sources are acquired and/or arranged for students.*

Teachers, principals, school and public librarians, local media sources, and various community agencies and businesses work together to provide students with a broad range of informational and technical materials. Improved access to Internet sources at home, in school, at libraries, and at workplaces provides great opportunities for the inquiring minds of middle-grade students. Individuals living in each community are also valuable sources of information, so students learn interviewing protocols and data-gathering strategies and interviews are arranged.

- *Documentation is arranged for being accountable to district and state learning goals, and ways to assess growth in reading, writing, speaking, and listening are created.*

Current accountability concerns about student achievement and increased surveillance of schools have caused teachers to implement activities that combine teaching and assessment. Rubrics, checklists, student products and portfolios are some of the ways teachers demonstrate student growth and achievement in literacy skills. Other teachers key student literacy outcomes to district and state learning goals that say students will use language arts to acquire, assess, and communicate information. To assess students the teachers create checklists for documenting how learning outcomes match thematic unit learning activities.

- *Content and literacy area lessons are combined to provide time blocks for information literacy activities.*

Given that the curriculum is already overloaded, time is always a prime concern. To make time for applied literacy lessons teachers combine reading, writing, language arts, and spelling schedules with science and social studies time slots. The combination of time, content, and the opportunity to use all of the language arts processes (speaking, listening, reading, writing) allows students' questions and concerns to drive the learning process.

- *Concepts and themes are used to integrate content areas with reading, writing, speaking, and listening activities.*

There is some evidence and plenty of teacher opinion to back up the idea that student motivation, engagement, and thinking are enhanced when learning activities are organized around concepts and themes. Common topics provide students with handles and hooks for their questions and concerns to both content and literacy strategies. Most conceptual and thematic information literacy apprenticeships are conducted on a single-classroom basis, although grade-level, and even schoolwide, thematic studies are possible.

- *Cooperative learning groups are arranged.*

When students work together they are often more engaged as learners, so teachers organize teams of students who select topics, pose questions, and target areas of inquiry. Teachers show students examples of the reports they could produce and present to real audiences of students, parents, and community groups. Teachers also group students heterogeneously by ability and model cooperative learning activities that stress sharing and evaluating information.

- *Whole-class teaching is used to generate questions and interest, model strategies, and manage the apprenticeships.*

Teachers initiate interest in themes and concepts by reading aloud, sharing stories, and displaying various sources of informational materials. In whole-class discussions the teacher and students brainstorm possible avenues of inquiry and make lists of names, topics, questions, issues. Using the chalkboard, large newsprint, and overhead projectors teachers help students organize the names, topics, questions, and so forth into meaningful categories that match students' names and student teams with topics and questions. These visual arrays are basic scaffolds teachers and students use to relate topics and questions to student interests and concerns. Teachers and students share the responsibility for time lines and scheduling learning activities.

- *Visual arrays and formats are necessary for organizing, thinking about, and communicating.*

Information by itself does not automatically engage students, so teachers provide formats like semantic maps and visual formats for putting facts and information into meaningful arrangements and useful contexts. Sorting information into categories like cause and effect, before and after, same and different, known information and new information, or fact and opinion gives meaning to content and ideas. Teachers report that arranging information into two-column compare-and-contrast charts triggers critical thinking and helps students organize written reports and oral presentations.

- *Content literacy minilessons are used to motivate, support, and guide student inquiry.*

As groups of students begin to read, discuss, gather information, and as they attempt to write, edit, and publish reports, teachers conduct minilessons.

Minilessons are taught on an as-needed basis. Sometimes teachers anticipated the need for a minilesson, for example, a vocabulary lesson, if they suspected students were having difficulty with unfamiliar words. At other times a minilesson on writing summaries was called for in response to a concern about main ideas and details. Teachers report that these content literacy minilessons "take" because students apply them immediately as they read, write, discuss, edit, revise, publish, and present reports.

- *A variety of communicating arrangements are employed.*

In addition to typical written and oral reports, students use a variety of communication modes. They include, but are not limited to, the following: written reports, illustrated oral reports, newspaper and television news formats, panels and debates, audio and video technologies, and technology-based Web pages and E-mail.

This list defines applied literacy. All nine practices are the significant features of lessons that help middle-grade students experience how to use their literacy skills for a variety of social and academic purposes.

Reading and Writing Like an Adult in the Middle Grades

The rest of this book expands on the ideas and activities I've just listed and describes them in more detail. My hope is that you will find the information useful for helping curious and energetic children learn as they figure things out from the inside by constructing new texts. As literate adults we choose what we read depending on our specific individual and social needs. So we read for enjoyment, or inquiry, or informational reasons. At work we often work together on projects and we have to share information, discuss what we know, and decide what to do with it. We use reading, writing, speaking, and listening to construct our own texts that help us satisfy our curiosity, make decisions, and learn new skills. So did sixth-grader Karen, who is mentioned in the first vignette at the beginning of this chapter. Her teacher organized a science biography unit and Karen was inspired by the real story of woman scientist Gertrude Elion. Elion was repeatedly denied work as a cancer researcher, only to eventually win the Nobel prize in 1988 for all the cancer-fighting drugs she developed. Karen's encounter with Elion's life story revealed why many productive women scientists were omitted from the time line of famous inventors and scientists. The applied literacy activities arranged by Karen's teacher "lit the fire" that led Karen to engage in authentic and practical learning. With plenty of help from her peers and her teachers, Karen acted like a literate adult as she acquired, assessed, and used social studies and science information that was interesting, important, and relevant to both her and her friends' personal concerns.

Summary

Vignettes, ideas on multiple literacies, children's and teachers' comments, and classroom examples were used to introduce applied literacy and argue for its value in the middle grades. Many of the separate teaching ideas in this chapter are not new. When teachers combine them, however, they create a classroom that takes full advantage of middle-grade children's curiosity and energy for learning. Because children in these grades are novice learners, teachers have to provide plenty of help, guidance, and support. The rest of the book describes in more detail what this type of teaching entails.

In addition to particular applied literacy teaching strategies, there are some larger curriculum, staffing, and community issues. The next chapter explains how applied literacy fits into a balanced school literacy curriculum, and describes some basic classroom contexts that support authentic inquiry.

References

Apple, M., & Beane, J. (1995). *Democratic Schools.* Alexandria, VA: Association for Supervision and Curriculum Development.

Bean, T. W., Bean, S. K., & Bean, K. F. (1999). Intergenerational conversations and two adolescents' multiple literacies: Implications for redefining content area literacy. *Journal of Adolescent & Adult Literacy, 42,* 438–448.

Borges, J. L. (1990). In S. Gilbar (Ed.), *The reader's quotation book.* New York: Barnes & Noble, 158.

Brooks, T. (1998). Back to the tracks. On *Back to the tracks* [CD]. New York: Blue Note Records, CDP-21737. (Track 1, Recorded October 20, 1960).

Elley, R. (1992). *How in the world do students read?* The Hague: International Association for the Evaluation of Educational Achievement.

Gee, J. (1996). *Social linguistics and literacies* (2nd ed.). Bristol, PA: Falmer Press.

Gee, J. (1999). Reading versus reading something: A critique of the National Academy of Sciences Report on Reading. In R. Telfer (Ed.), *Literacy Conversations: Family, School, Community: Nineteenth Yearbook of the American Reading Forum* (pp.1–12). Whitewater, WI: Publisher.

Guthrie, J. T., & Wigfield, A. (1997). *Motivating readers through integrated instruction.* Newark, DE: International Reading Association.

Manzo, A. V., & Manzo, U. C. (1995). *Teaching children to be literate.* Orlando, FL: Holt, Rinehart and Winston.

Moore, D. W., Bean, T. W., Birdyshaw, D. & Rycik, J. A. (1999, September). Adolescent literacy: A position statement. *Journal of Adult and Adolescent Literacy 43,* 97–112.

Stille, D. R. 1995. *Extraordinary women scientists.* Chicago: Childrens Press.

Turvey, P. 1994. *Inventors and ingenious ideas.* New York: Franklin Watts.

Vare, E. A., & Ptacek, M. (1993). *Women inventors and their discoveries.* Minneapolis: Oliver Press.

2

Applied Literacy in Your School and Classroom

We know that students bring the desires for involvement, curiosity, social interaction, challenge, and enhancement of self-efficiency into school activities. If the context supports these motivational goals, students become intensively involved. If the context suppresses them, children become disaffected.

J. Guthrie, 1996, p. 436

To better help you understand what this book is all about I want you to step back and take a panoramic view of applied literacy. The first part of this chapter describes how I believe applied literacy fits into the larger school curriculum. In the second part I discuss how teachers create a classroom context that supports applied literacy and then illustrate such a context with a thematic unit on local unsung heroes.

School Literacy: A Question of Balance

At the start of the new millennium school literacy programs are a battleground for heated debate among extremists jockeying for control of content, teaching methods, teacher preparation, and professional development. In the 1990s the cry to provide balanced literacy instruction ascended like a dove of peace from the smoke of the reading wars. It is unfortunate that the fight is most commonly known as a battle between whole-language zealots and lovers of phonics. The unfortunate part of this is that the reading wars battle scene is too complex to simply label one side whole language and the other phonics. Instead we need a more complex and detailed diorama to see how the applied literacy puzzle pieces fit together and relate to the larger school literacy curriculum.

One such curricular diorama that I subscribe to is Pearson and Raphael's (1999) continuum model of the *context* and *content* of literacy instruction (see Figure 2.1). Arguing that a balanced curriculum has "many independent elements that must be simultaneously balanced," they identify four *context* factors—authenticity, classroom discourse, teacher roles, and curricular control, and three *content* factors—skill contextualization, text genres, and response to literature. Each of these is akin to a scale that can be tipped from one extreme to another. For example, in the following continuum figure notice how the factor of authenticity can be tipped toward unrealistic "school-only" tasks like counting syllables in lists of words or toward "real-life" tasks like using letters and E-mail to get information from an interesting and reliable source. It's hard to argue against authenticity, but the truth is that students need both school skills and life skills. A balance of both is called for. The same idea of balance between teacher and student classroom discourse, or talk, is called for, depending on the literacy lesson.

I think you should get the picture by now so that it makes sense to discuss how applied literacy tips the scales of each factor.

Authenticity

The words *applied literacy* were chosen to clearly communicate that these activities are tipped toward out-of-school and real-life applications. Applied literacy is, therefore, a piece of a literacy curriculum and should not be considered a complete school literacy package. While the inquiry process that underlies applied literacy has a powerful school or academic flavor, the lessons do not constitute a complete literacy curriculum. It is as much a mistake to balance all

Contextual Continuum		
Authenticity	School ···	Life
Classroom Discourse	Student ··	Teacher
Teacher Role	Minimal ··	Maximal
Curricular Control	Local ···	Distant

Content Continuum		
Skill Contextualization	Skill Driven ·······························	Context Driven
Text Genres	Narrative/Practice ····················	Expository/Authentic
Response to Text	Efferent ·······································	Aesthetic

FIGURE 2.1

literacy learning on the back of applied literacy activities and nonfiction text as it is foolish to balance all literacy learning on the back of artists–authors who produce excellent fiction.

Classroom Discourse

Applied literacy lessons allow for many different patterns of control over topics and turn-taking. Sometimes the teacher will control both, such as during mini-lessons that feature direct instruction and modeling. Sometimes teachers and students will share control as they brainstorm subtopics and decide what questions to answer and who will be responsible for gathering information on subtopics. At other times students will control both, such as when they are communicating information after writing a report or acting out a scene from history. Ideally, classroom discourse will be balanced across the continuum of direct teacher guidance and support to student control of topics and turn-taking.

Teacher Role

This factor is closely related to the discourse factors of control topics and turn-taking, but focuses more directly on levels of teacher control and student activity during instruction. Applied literacy lessons call for the use of all five teacher roles that are marked by a release of teacher control and an increase in student activity. On one end of the scale is *explicit instruction,* when teacher control is high and student activity is low. Moving down on the scale toward less teacher control and more activity by students are *modeling,* then *scaffolding,* then *facilitating,* and, finally, *full participation.* Successful applied literacy activities require all five teacher roles. If teachers remain in control students may not be able to pursue topics of interest and may not be engaged. On the other hand, if teachers abandon students to the library with a simple "Do a report on whatever" directive, students will flounder.

Curricular Control

Applied literacy activities are tilted toward local control of the vehicle for inquiry activities, so those who most intimately know the students control the themes, topics, questions, and ways of sharing and communicating information. However, there are standards and benchmarks that are controlled by those who do not know the local community, the students, and the teachers. Curricular balance can be achieved if the parents and teachers, who know the students the best, make it clear how applied literacy learning relates to mandated benchmarks. However, if those who know the students least mandate specific methods and materials, there is a danger that applied literacy activities could be either mandated or prohibited, a situation no one needs.

Skill Contextualization

Applied literacy lessons clearly tip the scales toward contextually driven skill lessons. In other words, literacy skills are taught during the "teachable moment" or when they are needed to learn from a text or complete a learning activity. The vocabulary and comprehension minilessons described in Chapter 8 are clearly tied to the contexts dictated more by texts, learning tasks, and immediate student needs than by a preplanned scope and sequence. The assumption is that teachers will recognize the need for minilessons and provide direct instruction, scaffolding, modeling, or review and practice at a time when the skill will apply. This is an "ideal" notion that can backfire. It assumes teachers are attentive and caring and know what skills to teach and how to teach them. If teachers are not attentive to student needs or do not know or care about specific skills, students can be short-changed. Skill contextualization is a moral issue. If you choose to try applied literacy activities with a theme, multiple sources, and an inquiry process, you are morally bound to include skill lessons because your middle-grade students are novices who need plenty of timely instruction.

Text Genres

Applied literacy definitely favors expository over narrative, primary sources over essays, descriptions over poetry. Related narratives and stories are sometimes included but practice material like workbooks and textbooks with preloaded vocabulary and comprehension activities are rarely featured. Applied literacy activities are an attempt to balance a school literacy genre scale that quite frankly has favored narrative text in the past. There is evidence from both national and state tests that students experience more difficulties reading expository text than when they read narrative. This is one of the main reasons applied literacy lessons are needed in the middle grades. In terms of balance students obviously need a literary diet that includes both narrative and expository text.

Response to Text

How readers respond to text is related to their decision to take an efferent or an aesthetic stance toward the text (Rosenblatt, 1978). When we read we choose how we respond. We can take an aesthetic stance when we focus on our feelings and reactions to the problems, conflicts, and emotions that unfold in the story, poem, or whatever text we hold in our hand. We can also take an efferent stance and focus on how we might use the information and ideas after we encounter them in the text or source. Often we slip back and forth on this scale, depending on our purpose, the writer's intent, and the literacy event we are experiencing.

Applied literacy lessons tend to favor an efferent stance as readers actively, and I might add hopefully, attempt to get information from a nonfiction source to solve a problem, answer a question, or understand phenomena. However, readers are free to adopt any kind of stance with any kind of text. This means response stances are reader-, and, to some extent, teacher-, controlled. So, while applied literacy favors an efferent stance to texts and sources, students can respond aesthetically when nonfiction texts, events, and information trigger feelings and emotions.

Response to text is a lightning rod that attracts debate over the two basic goals of schooling. One goal is that schools exist to pass on the conventions—the culture, lore, history, as well as the language and civilized patterns—that allow us to live together. The other impelling goal for schools is to prepare students to become inventors—adults who will be able to live in a world that is yet to be. At first blush, applied literacy lessons are often advertised as though they are tools needed for constructing the future. However, applied literacy lessons can also help students see how and why the valued conventions from the past were constructed. In that sense applied literacy activities can help balance the tension between the twin purposes of education—looking back and looking ahead.

A balanced school literacy curriculum includes applied literacy activities that have both immediate and long-range benefits. The school context I just described introduces children to authentic inquiry and in doing so engages and motivates them in their formative years by providing them with authentic literacy experiences.

Your Classroom: A Context for Authentic Inquiry

When I observe effective applied literacy lessons I find teachers borrowing, adapting, and, in a real sense, inventing ways for their students to engage in authentic inquiry. The classroom contexts they construct feature three powerful elements:

- Student motivation and engagement has direct lines to *concept-oriented reading instruction* (Guthrie, 1996).
- Teacher organization and management have the structure and the flavor of *themed studies* (Reutzel & Cooter, 2000).
- The teaching strategies and instructional activities feature *content literacy activities* (McKenna & Robinson, 1997).

In the discussion that follows I will illustrate how these elements are played out in a sixth-grade themed study of "unsung heroes."

Motivation and Engagement

The renewed focus on student motivation and interest has been prompted by the realization that living and working in the information age require higher-order thinking skills that go beyond decoding and comprehending text. Critical reading skills—identifying problems, searching for information from multiple sources, questioning the validity of sources, applying prior knowledge to texts, generating inferences, and linking information across genres—are not learned well unless individuals are highly motivated. A promising teaching plan that supports motivation and engagement and leads students to higher-order literacy skills is the Concept-Oriented-Reading-Instruction (CORI) model (Guthrie, 1996). Students find CORI engaging because they choose topics and questions themselves, they are often challenged but not overwhelmed by the reading and writing, and they talk, write, and gain information in a social manner with teams of peers. To illustrate this idea I have constructed a sixth-grade "unsung heroes" unit that features several CORI practices: direct observation, multiple conceptual themes, and small-group learning that features self-direction and collaboration.

Direct Observation.   In addition to interacting with traditional secondary sources such as print, media, pictures, or models of reality, students observe, collect, touch, handle real objects, and talk with real people. For example, with the theme study of local unsung heroes, students talk to (interview) people from the community who contribute to community life. They interview workers at a recycling center. They ask municipal workers who operate the water treatment plan to find out how they make sure the water is safe, clear, and tastes good. Direct contact with primary sources arouses interest and often leads students to immediately ask good questions that get at "why" and "how" and issues like "importance," or concerns like "is the work hard or what problems are hardest to solve"?

Concepts and Themes.   When students connect information from prior knowledge, direct observation, and multiple texts, they are more likely to be engaged and motivated. One reason for this is that higher-order thinking kicks in when information is more readily linked by compare and contrast or cause and effect. This motivates students because they can more easily generate explanations for what they have observed. For example, when students combine firsthand experiences with water (drinking, bathing, playing), a discussion with clean and waste water treatment workers, an observation of a wastewater treatment plant, and their reading of a nonfiction book about Diane Schindler, a worker at a wastewater treatment plant (*Who Keeps the Water Clean? Ms. Schindler*, by Duvall, 1997), they understand how particular people in a community contribute to the greater good. They also experience how science is applied in wastewater treatment and how they can see firsthand how taxes support technical and human resources to control pollution in wastewater.

Self-Direction and Collaboration.   An important feature of applied literacy that CORI follows is that individual students get to personalize their efforts and share, listen, help, and learn from others. For example, students may not all be interested in wastewater treatment work so they seek other local sites where people make a contribution to the community with their work or volunteer activities. However, complete student autonomy to pursue topics is not possible. The teacher must be able to provide resources for students to have direct observation as well as enough secondary sources to allow for some in-depth study of a topic. For example, one way teachers give students choices is to have a variety (you never can have enough) of texts that can help students think of other situations where local heroes quietly go about their tasks. Consider the choices provided by the following nonfiction books from Children's Press, and you can see how pairs or trios of students might use them as a focus for direct observation and study that is part of the local hero theme.

- *Dr. Friedman Helps Animals* by Flanagan 1999. The work of veterinarian Ellen Friedman is shown in photos and text.

- *Mr. Paul and Mr. Luecke Build Communities* by Flanagan 1999. A photo and text look at the work of home building contractors.

- *Working At A TV Station* by Davis 1998. *Working At A Museum* by L'Hommedieu 1998. *Working At A Zoo* by Knight 1998. *Working At A Marine Institute* by Davis 1998. These are all part of a series of photos plus text sources called Working Here.

While not all local communities have a zoo or a marine institute, the idea is to brainstorm places and people in the local area that students find interesting. For example, study the following graphic organizer and try to list people in each of the five sections who are local workers or volunteers who contribute to the community (Figure 2.2).

Some people who come to mind might be the local blood drive director, a business owner who hires disabled individuals, a director of a shelter for homeless people, or a city worker who plows snow in the winter. Whatever choices are made, students can work singly or in pairs and small teams to gather information about the work involved. As they find out why, what, when, and how people do what they do, they will uncover a host of interesting details and issues to talk and write about.

FIGURE 2.2

Collaboration in small groups is engaging and helps students construct meaning when information from multiple sources like interviews, observations, and nonfiction sources (text, media, Internet) are discussed during the "idea circle" (Guthrie, 1996, p. 439). During these discussions students not only press each other for details and explanations, they encourage each other to search for more information. They also learn discussion skills when teachers prompt them to take turns, listen, speak one at a time, and stay on the topic. The intent is that sixth graders will share information from interviews and picture books and they will be motivated to publish their own books featuring pictures and texts of local unsung heroes.

Organization and Management

Applied literacy activities in the middle grades are best organized around in-depth studies that last two or three weeks in grades three through five and up to five or six weeks in grades six through eight. The planning phases for organizing themed studies tend to flow from *theme selection,* to setting educational *goals and objectives,* to *webbing the subtopics* with the theme, to selecting *learning activities and materials* and to *fine tuning* to decide specifics about time, student teams, assignments, and a host of paper and pencil tasks. The organization and management of the "Unsung Heroes" involved several different activities.

Theme Selection.   In addition to motivating students, themed studies are a way to organize information into categories in order to establish order, arrange routines, and keep track of who is doing what. Theme studies are a lot of work so teachers try to plan activities so students will be able to gather information from plenty of primary and secondary sources. The unsung heroes theme appears manageable. The concept is familiar to students because local news media do a weekly story on people who, although relatively unrecognized by mass media, have made or are making important contributions to others. The teacher selected this theme because it allows students to do biography studies in many areas including the sciences, social services, government, education, and business. In addition to learning about unsung heroes from anywhere and anytime, students can include local people whose efforts contribute to the quality of life in the local community.

In this example I talk about a single teacher. However, teams of teachers often do themed studies. Just as theme study "tends to connect informational dots into more vivid images" (Manzo, Manzo, & Estes, 2001, p. 380), teachers from different content areas often collaborate to weave together information from a variety of sources. The result is that students see the whole cloth, not just the separate threads.

Setting Goals and Objectives.   In addition to the special content learned in a themed study, the teacher focused on meeting local and state reading and language arts and social studies objectives. Establishing goals and objectives that are directly related to mandated local and state curriculum goals is a highly professional act that demonstrates to the community how educational accountability works in the information age.

For example, when students interview local heroes they use speaking, listening, and writing and demonstrate that they can use the language arts processes to gain new content information in science and social studies from secondary and primary sources. Students also use reading and reference skills to gather information from secondary sources. They combine the information from interviews and text sources to write reports about people who, although relatively unknown, have made significant contributions in government, social services, business, and education. Through their reading, interviewing, and reporting activities, students produce evidence that they can read, listen, take notes, and write descriptive reports. The unsung hero theme also promotes the use of biographic performance activities in which students produce audio- and video-based reports that are modeled after current media formats they encounter in the popular culture, such as radio and television talk shows and news media special reports like those they see in newspapers and television.

As you can see, a thematic approach is challenging and risky. Instead of a simple single text that all students study, a teacher works with students to create a unique set of objectives, topics, questions, student products, primary and secondary sources, as well as learning outcomes. Because this has the potential to be either engaging and productive, or disorganized and frustrating, there is a need for *webbing* to set boundaries and fine-tuning to keep students on target.

Webbing Subtopics.   In order for students and teachers to see the global "big picture," the next step was to create a schema map to illustrate the links between the different sections of the themed study. The map or web is flexible and can be revised when new information and insights prompt the teacher and the students to move the pieces around. Figure 2.3 illustrates an initial web for the unsung hero theme.

This Web is not fully developed but it shows how the theme spans science and social studies.

Learning Activities and Materials.   The unsung hero unit allows for great flexibility in materials, sources of information, as well as activities that demonstrate that students can apply their language arts skills to gain new information in science and social studies. Students read expository text and interview people whose work has quietly contributed to better government, safer communities, a cleaner environment, better medicine and medical care, or a better understanding of natural phenomenon. They learn about problems these individuals encountered and find out what motivated them to do what they do. Students demonstrate learning by preparing and presenting written reports and visual displays, as well as oral reports or short skits that both inform and entertain.

One does not have to think hard to see that themed studies require plenty of diverse materials and information sources. In addition to lots and lots of non-

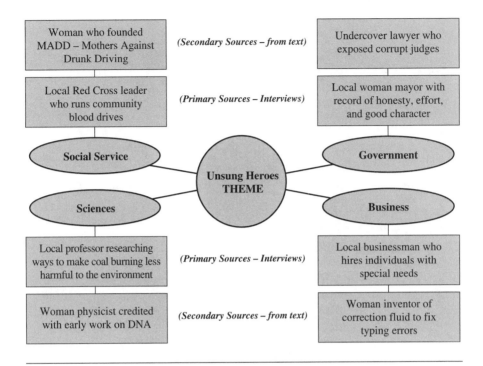

FIGURE 2.3

fiction books and reference sources, students will need access to the Internet, as well as directories, that help teachers and students find people to interview. In Chapter 4 information sources will be presented in more detail.

Fine-Tuning. There seem to be a thousand details to consider with themed studies. How long should the study last? Exactly what questions will students tackle and what materials will they use? Which teaching and reporting activities will teachers and students use? In addition, when students get started, the teachers will have to decide how much scaffolding is necessary, which minilessons the students will need, and when it will be best to present them.

One fine-tuning decision for teachers is how to sequence the unit activities. In a self-contained classroom a teacher can spend one week on the science part of the unit and another week on the social studies segment or even run them concurrently. Another sequence is to have some students pursuing science segments and others social studies segments. This approach has the advantage of being like an adult workplace in which literacy skills and content study are fully integrated during the school day and student engagement and interest are often sustained.

However, many middle-grade classrooms are departmentalized so that social studies and science are separated because different content specialists teach subjects. In this situation different teachers do separate themed studies that last from two to four weeks. In some departmentalized situations teachers are able to plan together and do concurrent themes that share topics, activities, materials, and outcomes. They try to start and finish their themed studies at the same time to prevent confusion and interference that can sap interest.

In other situations teams of teachers at one grade level do integrated themed studies that cut across all of the content subjects so that students study science, social studies, math, language arts, and even art and music under an umbrella theme. This approach is rare because, when teachers try to agree on so many key elements, they can feel compromised and controlled. Furthermore, full integration takes a great deal of planning time as well as frequent contact to manage and fine-tune lessons and activities. In most schools teachers have a choice about how they will operate, so not all content teachers will be equally ready to do integrated themed studies.

Regardless of whether teachers operate in a self-contained or a departmentalized situation, the final details of managing themed units requires daily planning. To do this teachers plan a time line, specify the individual and group writing and reporting tasks, select minilessons and teaching techniques, and provide primary and secondary sources for students. Many of the details are decided after the themed study is started because students will encounter new information. New information can raise new questions or change the direction of inquiry. This openness and willingness to alter ideas and tasks in the face of new information is a hallmark of the climate and spirit of true inquiry. A detailed plan for a science segment of the unsung heroes theme illustrates the kind of planning required.

Unsung Heroes—The Science Segment

Individual research tasks
- Each student selects two scientists and takes notes using the "I-Search Process" (Macrorie, 1988).
- Three to four days of writing workshop class time is provided.

Group writing tasks
- Pairs of students combine notes and write a report on the "unknown" scientists they have selected.
- Three to four days of class time is allowed.
- Teacher provides minilessons on report writing using summarization training (Rinehart, Stahl, & Erickson, 1986) and information charts (Randall, 1996).
- Writing workshop (prewriting, drafting, revising and editing, publishing) format (Calkins, 1994 and Atwell, 1987) is used.

Reporting tasks
- Student pairs present reports using two formats.
- Three to four days of class time is allowed.
- Format A: Two students become an unsung hero and tell their stories as though they were talking "live" on television. Parents are invited.

- Format B: Students take turns reading their reports to an audience of students in other classes. Reports are illustrated with posters.

Primary Sources

Teacher helps students contact scientists at local university who are involved with interesting applications of science. Some local businesses may also be sources for people who are applying science technology in a fashion deemed worthy of recognition as unsung heroes. For example, students might interview the manager of the local municipal water treatment plant or wastewater treatment plant and describe how science is used to treat water before and after it is used in the community. Students could interview directors of a local recycling center and find out where glass, aluminum, plastic, and paper go and how each is processed and reused.

Secondary Sources

Extraordinary Woman Scientists (Stille, 1995) Childrens Press.
Women Inventors and Their Discoveries (Vare & Ptacek, 1993) Oliver Press.
Inventions: Inventors and Ingenious Ideas (Turvey, 1994) Franklin Watts.

Instructional Strategies

As rookie researchers, middle-grade students benefit from content literacy strategies that teachers provide when students need them during the inquiry process. Because it is hard to judge ahead of time exactly which teaching strategies will help the most, teachers have to be ready with content literacy strategies they can teach "on the fly" when students need help. This means teachers have to be prepared with a small arsenal of techniques for helping students. A basic list of these techniques includes:

- Selecting and Defining Topics
- Asking Good Questions
- Learning New Vocabulary
- Interviewing Sources
- Comprehending/Organizing Information
- Writing and Presenting Reports

Selecting and Defining Topics.   A cardinal rule for initiating a discussion and inquiry is to start with a specific and concrete opener that leads to a theme or general topic. For example, when starting a discussion and inquiry into a "local heroes" theme, start with specific people who exemplify the theme. One idea is to have a real-life local hero speak to the class and answer student questions. Another technique is to use existing books and challenge students to do their own version. For example, show students several biography books and ask, "What local people are like the people in these books?" The book *A Female Focus: Great Women Photographers* (Horwitz, 1996) may prompt students to interview a local press photographer whose photos often accompany local news stories. *Extraordinary People with Disabilities* (Kent & Quinlan, 1996) may lead students to look for local heroes with disabilities. Others may decide to interview local home builders after looking over the book *Mr. Paul and Mr. Leucke Build Communities* (Flanagan, 1999). The picture books are concrete examples that provide a model for the students. The trick here is to convince students that they can produce their own books that will feature their own photos of the local heroes as well as the text they write based on the information they gather from interviews, brochures, and other print sources they encounter along the way.

Asking Good Questions.   Because inquiry is based on questions, teachers need to spend time helping novice researchers ask questions that lead to new and interesting information. One teacher (Tower, 2000) reported that she needed to spend more time than she initially allowed for students to generate good inquiry questions. She did use K-W-L charts but the student questions were very factual and often had one answer that was easy to locate. Students asked "small" questions such as "What do moles eat?" She had to organize lessons that helped them ask meaningful and large questions like "Why are moles a problem?" and "What are some ways to control moles?" To do this she used some good student questions as models and told her students:

> To ask what a tiger eats is too small. *Here's an example of a big question.* Should tigers be allowed to be in the circus? *This question doesn't have one right answer; people will disagree about this question (p. 552).*

The following table provides a compare/contrast content literacy teaching idea that can help students ask "big" questions that do not have a single or simple answer. To do this prepare a list of "small" questions with accompanying "big" questions to model the kind of thinking needed for authentic inquiry.

Small Questions: One Answer	Big Questions: Several Answers
What do moles eat?	What problems do moles cause?
What do lions eat?	Should lions be in the circus?
Where do deer live?	What problems do deer cause?
What was a knight's body armor made of?	How has body armor changed from the middle ages to now?

Discuss the differences between the two, and ask students to generate other examples.

Small Questions	Big Questions
_____	_____
_____	_____
_____	_____
_____	_____

After students have made their lists, have a whole-class discussion about asking broad questions that require more than one answer.

Learning New Vocabulary.   When students begin their inquiry, they may encounter new vocabulary as they read nonfiction for background information. For example, students reading about photography will encounter technical words such as *composition, photomontage,* and *syncroflash.* To help them the teacher can teach the words directly by showing the whole class how to make word cards. This technique helps students understand new terms, use them in their interviews, explain them to their classmates, and use them in their own writing. Figure 2.4 illustrates the word card for *composition.*

Interviewing.   Interviewing adults is often intimidating and students often wonder what questions they might ask. Interview prompt cards can help with this. The teacher can have a whole-class lesson on interview questions that culminates with each student creating an interview prompt card. On their cards, students can list key questions and prompts they might use when they are conducting their interviews. The teacher tells the students how she often jots down a list of questions when she goes to talk with her doctor, the principal, or anytime she needs important information. The question prompt card idea may lead the students who are interviewing the homebuilders to write these questions on their card:

- How did you decide to be a homebuilder?
- What do you like best about your work?

(front of card)

	noun
composition	

(Back of card)

definition	*in photography: the arrangement and relationship among all of the objects in the picture.*
synonym	*pattern, combination, style of picture.*
sentences	*The happy composition featured faces of four laughing children.*

FIGURE 2.4

- Is there any part of your work you dislike?
- Is the work hard, dangerous, exciting, boring, easy?
- How do you feel when you finish building a home for someone?
- Did anybody ever get mad at you for building a home for them?
- How do you decide what people should pay you for building a home for them?

Comprehending and Organizing Information. When students are seeking information by reading, searching the Internet, or conducting interviews, the teacher is prepared to help students when they encounter problems with taking notes, summarizing and organizing ideas, writing and editing drafts, and preparing reports.

For example, if students interview two homebuilders, the teacher can help them construct an expository chart to summarize and organize their information. In the following sixth-grade example, two students, Mark and Shawn, talked to homebuilder Jeff Simpson. Mr. Simpson, a friend of Mark's family, agreed to talk with the two boys after a pizza dinner at Mark's home. The other builder, Norm Otto, talked on the telephone with the boys and they captured the interview on a tape recorder. The boys used the question prompt card for both interviews, tried to take notes when they talked with Mr. Simpson, and taped Mr. Otto's responses. It was hard to write everything down that Mr. Simpson said and they could not transcribe the tape recording, so the day after the interviews they worked together to complete the following chart using their incomplete notes and the recording.

Topic/Sources	*Question 1*	*Question 2*	*Question 3*	*Question 4*
Local Unsung Heroes—Home Builders.	How did you decide to be a homebuilder?	What do you like best about your work?	What is the hardest part of your work?	How do you decide what people should pay you for a home?
S-1	*S-1, Q-1*	*S-1, Q-2*	*S-1, Q-3*	*S-1, Q-4*
Owner of a construction company, Mr. Sawyer.	family business started in 1950s by grandfather	the work of building itself—the measuring, sawing, nailing	finding and keeping good carpenters and workers	knows what materials cost and what labor costs so he can tell by the size and kind of materials.

S-2	S-2, Q-1	S-2, Q-2	S-2, Q-3	S-2, Q-4
Mr. Otto, Manager of Prestige Homes.	started as an electrician	planning a home with buyers, new customers	meeting all the laws, codes, and rules that must be followed	

Writing and Reporting.   There are many stages in the inquiry process and students move at different rates and with different levels of intensity. In order to allow students to work at their own pace, the teacher has to watch the writing and reporting carefully to help them through the long haul from initial idea to final product.

Expository maps like the previous example are one strategy that teachers use to help students with writing and reporting. The teacher uses the questions and notes and "collects" them in a vertical fashion and shows students how sentences can be developed by combining questions and notes. For example, the teacher combines question 3 on the hardest parts of a home builder's work with the responses from two contractors and writes:

> *Some of the hardest parts of a home builder's job are finding and keeping good workers and following all the building codes and rules.*

Checklists for speaking are another strategy teachers use to help students present reports. After their reports are written, students can practice presenting them using the speaking checklist in Box 2.1, which will help them be better communicators.

BOX 2.1

Format and Style—While talking, I will:

_____   use information from my written report
_____   prepare a three-minute talk about what I learned
_____   have good eye contact and a friendly look on my face
_____   use gestures, have good posture, look like I am having fun
_____   use a visual aid to illustrate and make ideas clear

Ideas and Content—I will:

_____   keep attention and interest of the audience with examples
_____   use my own words
_____   tell what I found most interesting

(continued)

Organization—My report will include:

_____ an interesting beginning
_____ details that illustrate important ideas
_____ an entertaining and memorable ending

Voice—During my talk I will:

_____ speak loudly, clearly, and at a rate that is understandable
_____ use good expression and my own style and personality
_____ watch the audience to see if I need to speak faster, slower, louder, quieter

Teacher Flexibility

By now it is apparent that teachers need to be flexible in order to manage an inquiry project undertaken by rookie researchers. Sometimes the teacher anticipates a problem and intervenes ahead of time with lessons like those I've just described. Sometimes the teacher is an observer who responds and intervenes with content literacy strategies when students encounter difficulties or when they ask for help. Teachers are prepared to accept the fact that some students will know more than they do about some topics and have better information seeking skills, especially on the Internet. Teachers know that some students need more help than others, and it is not unusual that some students are better sources of instructional help than the teacher. Instead of being out in front pulling or in back pushing, the teacher is comfortable working like a fishing guide standing next to students *with tips, directions, and expert advice.*

Knowing *when* to provide help to students is based on intuition, observation, and gut feeling. For example, sometimes a teacher anticipates a problem with difficult vocabulary and builds word meaning early into a themed study with definitions, context clues, synonyms, and concrete examples. At other times a problem is not discovered until students have gotten into difficulty answering questions or taking notes, so the teacher has to stop and teach how to infer and summarize. Because they are novice researchers, middle-grade students can falter, get off track, fail to find information, try to gather too much information, or lose interest. Teachers who anticipate these bumps and respond as best they can are prepared to respond with timely "repair" and "fix-up" teaching strategies that keep students moving ahead. Knowing *what* teaching strategies to use at any one time is based on experience and expertise and each teacher develops a "bag" of practical teaching ideas for helping students locate, assess, and use information from different sources. The bag holds examples and materials for teaching children to: ask "fat" questions, check the validity of sources, take notes, write summaries, and write reports.

Summary

In this chapter I describe how applied literacy fits into a school curriculum and gave an illustration of a classroom applied literacy unit on unsung heroes. One main point of this chapter is that applied literacy activities are part of a balanced school literacy curriculum. Another point is that applied literacy activities are not meant to replace all the excellent literacy lessons that already exist. A third point is that, in schools where I've observed applied literacy lessons, it is not implemented by all teachers on a schoolwide basis. Instead, different teachers in different subject matter areas created applied literacy units that made sense in the context of their particular curriculum with their particular students. The point is that middle-grade students benefit from applied literacy activities in different grades and in different content subjects.

In the next chapter student and teacher vignettes and detailed descriptions of the significant features of authentic inquiry are presented to help you gain a full understanding of applied literacy concepts.

References

Atwell, N. (1987). *In the middle: Writing, reading, and learning with adolescents.* Portsmouth, NH: Heineman.

Calkins, L. M. (1994). *The art of teaching writing* (new ed.). Portsmouth, NH: Heinemann.

Flanagan, A. K. (1999). *Mr. Paul and Mr. Leucke build communities.* Danbury, CT: Children's Press.

Guthrie, J. (1996). Educational contexts for engagement in literacy. *Reading Teacher, 49*(6), 432–445.

Horwitz, M. F. (1996). *A female focus: Great women photographers.* Danbury, CT: Franklin-Watts.

Kent, D., & Quinlan, K. (1996). *Extraordinary people with disabilities..* Danbury, CT: Children's Press.

Macrorie, K. (1988). *The I-Search paper.* Portsmouth, NH: Heinemann.

Manzo, A. V., Manzo, U. C., & Estes, T. H. (2001). *Content area literacy.* New York: John Wiley.

McKenna, M. C., & Robinson, R. D. (1997). *Teaching through text: A content literacy approach to content area reading* (2nd ed.). New York: Longman.

Pearson, P. D., & Raphael, T. E. (1999). Toward a more complex view of balance in the literacy curriculum. In W. D. Hammond & T. E. Raphael (Eds.), *Early literacy instruction for the new millennium* (pp. 1–21). Grand Rapids, MI: Michigan Reading Association, Center for the Improvement of Early Reading Achievement.

Randall, S. N. (1996). Informational charts: A strategy for organizing student research. *Journal of Adolescent & Adult Literacy, 39,* 536–542

Reutzel, D. R., & Cooter, R. B. (2000). *Teaching children to read.* Upper Saddle River, NJ: Merrill.

Rinehart, S., Stahl, S., & Erickson, L. G. (1986). Some affects of summarization training on reading and studying. *Reading Research Quarterly, 21*(4), 422–438.

Rosenblatt, L. (1978). *The reader, the text, the poem: The transactional theory of the literary work.* Carbondale, IL: Southern Illinois University Press.

Tower, C. (2000, April). Questions that matter: Preparing elementary students for the inquiry process. *Reading Teacher, 53*(7), 550–557.

3

Guiding Authentic Inquiry

These stories were extremely sophisticated. You wouldn't necessarily believe they were written by young kids.

B. Brown, Teacher

Applied literacy activities are grounded in authentic student interests, concerns, and experiences. In the following true vignette a seventh-grade student won a Young Author's Contest with a story that was prompted by a television documentary, her interest in history, her concern about the future, and her sister's modeling and encouragement.

Vignette

Grace, a seventh grader, was motivated to write her prize-winning twelve-chapter story by a PBS television documentary. The idea for Grace's story, "The Solitary Room," came from a PBS Nova episode about code breakers in World War II. Grace said, "My parents taped it and told me to watch it because it was so interesting. I was reluctant at first, but I thought it was a neat story." Grace took about a month to do research and write about a girl in the future who is transported back in time to become a code breaker during World War II.

In Grace's story the main character, Lysa Threnten, lives in a grim future where, in addition to harsh punishments, the ozone layer has been destroyed and there are no pets. In school, Lysa is caught passing a note. For punishment she is sent to the dreaded "Solitary Room" where one boy was sent five years before and never returned. When Lysa enters the room she drops her compubooks, trips, strikes her head, and becomes unconscious. When she awakes it is July 23, 1941 and she is in a lab where people are decoding Nazi messages. One of her fellow code breakers is Peter, the boy who disappeared five years earlier. Grace's story tells about code breaking, her experiences with Peter and other adults, and how Lysa gets out of the Solitary Room and back to her present life.

In a newspaper interview (Sickler, 2000), Grace says she is undecided about a career, but she "likes social studies because she likes history," and has "been trying to live up to my sister [who is a previous Young Authors winner]. She's the one who encourages me to write."

The vignette illustrates how a nonfiction documentary on the history of code breaking prompted Grace to combine history and code breaking information with her goal to be a writer like her sister and produce a story that put her into a life three hundred years in the future. Grace's writing was not only personally satisfying, it was judged to be useful, authentic, and worthy of praise by peers, teachers, and family.

Grace's experience reminded me of a favorite book on teaching, *In There with the Kids* by David Kobrin (1992). One of the main characters in the book is a teacher named Hillary, who uses seven questions when she plans units and lessons.

In my experience as a teacher I think that the first question on her list is not only the most important, it is also the most elusive. We are suspicious about trusting our students to be engaged enough to produce a high quality response to their own questions and concerns. It is easier for all of us as teachers to control what our students will have to do, what materials they'll use, and what their products will be. It is much harder to get our students to care, connect, and control their own learning.

Hillary keeps her questions in front of her at all times (under the glass top of her desk) because the care question is easy to overlook in the daily grind and fast pace of teaching (Figure 3.1, Kobrin, p. 55). Schoolwork forces teachers to be pragmatic and think mainly about materials, products, and grades, so it's no wonder we sometimes overlook whether or not the students care. One reason we move quickly over the caring part is the reality that getting students to care is always elusive, never guaranteed. All we can do is discipline ourselves to think,

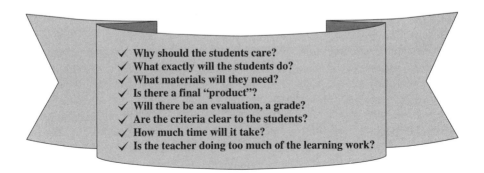

✓ Why should the students care?
✓ What exactly will the students do?
✓ What materials will they need?
✓ Is there a final "product"?
✓ Will there be an evaluation, a grade?
✓ Are the criteria clear to the students?
✓ How much time will it take?
✓ Is the teacher doing too much of the learning work?

FIGURE 3.1 *Why should the students care?*

"What kind of a plan can I devise so that my students may find this inquiry project useful to their lives?" Keep this question in mind as you read through the process for conducting authentic inquiry activities.

A Process for Conducting Authentic Inquiry

 Topics and Themes

There is no single "best practices" method for engaging students so that they "care" enough to participate in successful and satisfying inquiry projects. Sometimes a simple and loose arrangement that allows individual students or small teams of students to select different topics of interest, raise questions, collect and organize information, and produce oral and/or written reports works. However, there is often a trade-off between high initial interest and later low satisfaction due to unfocused topics, lack of nonfiction sources, and incomplete reports. Another problem with loosely organized inquiry is that students may select unclear or risky and inappropriate topics. And, when they are prevailed on to pursue a different issue, students often become disengaged from the entire inquiry project. Because of these pitfalls I recommend that teachers use more complex and structured arrangements on the front end because they will help avoid later problems with topics, sources, information, and products. In fact, when students have little experience with this process, teachers have found that it works better to do a single class-wide project than it is to let students try to do individual projects. Another good idea that helps novice researchers is for teachers to demonstrate how they researched a real topic of their own. After all, we are talking about novice researchers who, although highly curious about the world, lack formal inquiry experience.

Teachers who organize inquiry projects under broad thematic umbrellas report success using several favorite themes (Figure 3.2). Teachers also report that a timely or interesting theme, even though limiting in some respects, often increases student interest and motivation (Crosswhite, 1999).

Although there is mixed evidence that thematic studies are superior to single-text learning arrangements, there is plenty of anecdotal teacher support for integrating science, social studies, reading, and language arts. Teachers report that critical thinking is increased when students encounter alternative, and even contradictory, ideas and information on a topic. In addition, with a thematic arrangement students discuss, compare, and share information across topics. Finally, the most compelling argument for thematic studies is teacher reports of high student enthusiasm, creativity, and sustained effort.

 Issues and Questions

Here is where the usefulness of a broad theme begins to pay off by providing different "handles" or specific questions to engage student interest. One of the key ingredients to engaging students is giving them a say in what they will study. A

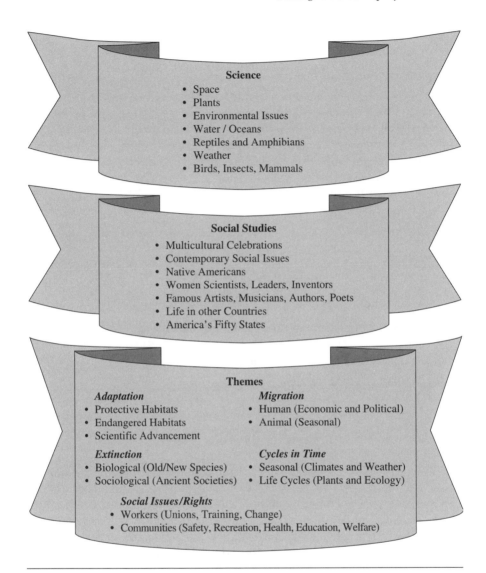

FIGURE 3.2

good way to do this is to have a whole-class discussion and brainstorming session using questions to focus the discussion.

- Why is this topic important?
- What is happening in the world around us that is related to this topic?
- What do we already know about the topic?
- What are some things we'd like to know?

- Who else is interested in this topic?
- Who might find information on this topic useful?
- Who are some audiences for information on this topic?

Teachers report that the *Know* and *Want-to-Know* sections of the KWL format (Ogle, 1986) are very useful for creating handles for students to grasp as subtopics as they investigate as individuals or as small groups. Teachers use the chalkboard, chart paper, or an overhead as they (or one of their students) record information and questions in the following format.

On the Topic or Theme of _____

    K—We know   **W**—Want to Know

Another format that works well for an initial whole-class discussion is a compare-and-contrast list. For example, to start a thematic study of life in other cultures a fourth-grade teacher had the class brainstorm a list of familiar features of life in the United States including examples of the following cultural items:

- Homes and community settings and arrangements
- Jobs and working patterns
- Marriage and family arrangements
- Food and eating practices
- Money and banking practices
- Transportation practices and patterns
- School and education patterns
- Government arrangements and services

The lists of items about life in the United States were categorized and discussed and the students were asked if they thought people in the other cultures they were studying had the same or different jobs, schools, food, and so on. This led the students to ask questions about the other cultures, which eventually became the focus of inquiry for teams of students. For example, under a subtopic about food and health in Japan they asked do they eat fast food in Japan? Or do they invest in a stock market in Japan?

In successful inquiry projects, teachers allow plenty of time for question development (Tower, 2000). Student questions will often reflect their common experience at looking for simple facts and straightforward information like, "What do moles eat?" This question has a narrow answer that can be supplied from one source. Teachers often have to intervene and lead students to ask broader questions like, "How can we prevent moles from damaging lawns and gardens?" This is a bigger question that has a variety of answers that people disagree about and information and possible answers will be found in several different sources.

The process of listing student ideas and questions is followed by grouping the ideas into categories and subtopics that they can select for inquiry. Matching subtopics to teams of students is a mixture of choosing and assigning: the teacher arbitrates as the students negotiate with each other to decide who will study what topics. This means that in a classroom of twenty-five or so students you will need a minimum of six to seven topical categories for teams of three to four students, or more categories for pairs and individuals to study. This process often takes more than one class session.

It is not unusual for some students to balk and not "care" to participate. Sometimes other students shun a student, which makes teaming him or her with other students a problem. The solution to these classroom problems ranges from gentle and successful persuasion to recording incidents of nonparticipation for parent conferencing and even special learning arrangements for noncompliant students. In the face of these problems, teachers report that it is best to carry on and work around instances when students either do not care about the theme or subtopics that were generated by the class discussions, or when students are socially isolated. A good rule of thumb is not to let one or more problem students stop the rest of the class. When I asked teachers about this problem, they said the most used solution was to assign a reluctant student to a motivated group. Sometimes they said they permitted noninvolved participants to pursue a special topic, which might or might not be related directly to the overall class theme, but this was a last resort.

The Inquiry Plan: Search Strategies and Data Sources

When students have selected a subtopic and have a clear notion of the question they are addressing, they then decide to begin looking for data. Very often teachers set some standards for inquiry. For example, each inquiry team is required to use three to five different sources such as books, articles, CD-ROMs, or Web sites. For some inquiry projects students may be required to interview knowledgeable community "experts." As students mature and gain inquiry experience, the need for minimum source requirements can diminish. In some cases students find "too much," so teachers have to put a limit on sources to meet time, writing, and reporting constraints.

At this point students often need help from teachers and media specialists to identify the key words and phrases that are needed to conduct a data search. Of course, the students need access to a variety of useful and accessible sources. Fortunately, many schools have well-stocked classroom and media center libraries. Unfortunately, many other schools have limited information sources. Because local information resources vary, each situation dictates its own search strategy. I've observed that, even in schools and small communities with virtually no library, teachers and students are conducting credible inquiry projects.

Often businesses and parents come to the rescue with magazines, books, home encyclopedia sets, and Internet connections. Local community "experts" are often excellent sources of information and provide students with productive and exciting interviewing experiences. Chapter 6 provides more information on data sources.

 ### Reading, Listening, Selecting, and Recording Data

When students begin reading, viewing a video, and/or interviewing a source, it is helpful to have the following "rules" or metacognitive questions posted in the classroom.

- Can I read/listen and understand the source?
- Does this information fit my objectives or answer my questions?
- Is the information accurate and authentic? Is the source reliable?

Other "rules" about how much information are also helpful to novice researchers. For example, in a fifth-grade class a pair of robins had built a nest on the outside ledge of a classroom window. The students had observed the nest building and they were excited by their opportunity for close observation. The teacher seized the moment and began reading *Flute's Journey* (Cherry, 1997), the story of a wood thrush's life. The story starts with a nest of four turquoise eggs, tells of Flute's early and mature life, and focuses on his annual migration from Maryland to Costa Rica. The students compared the wood thrush to the robins on their windowsill and began to talk, share information, and ask questions about all kinds of birds. The teacher suggested that for science and language arts teams of three students each would research and write a bird book. Teams were formed, a list of birds was generated, and each team selected a bird to study and write about. One "rule" the teacher set was that each student must find at least five pieces of information about the bird they were studying, and she gave each team packets of strips of paper. She told them that only one idea about their bird was to be written on one strip of paper.

The students met in their teams and began collecting information for their bird books by taking notes on the slips of paper. While some students groaned that finding five ideas was an impossible goal, others were able to produce a dozen or more in three days of reading and searching. When teams met they put all of their slips of paper on a table and the teacher helped them organize them into common categories such as what the bird eats, how many eggs it lays, what their nests look like, and so on. Each pile of common notes was labeled and the ideas on separate slips became the details in later paragraphs in the book. By using the strips of paper the children were less inclined to copy whole parts of text, and more inclined to write freely in their own words. And, because the strips were about one third of a standard-sized piece of paper, they could be organized by categories and kept in separate envelopes. The key to the successful note taking was the organization plan featuring slips of paper, one idea per slip, and envelopes for categorizing.

This was a very simple note taking plan for novice fifth-grade researchers. As students mature as researchers, the teacher can set more sophisticated note taking rules. For example, one idea, from Crosswhite (1999, p. 27), is to supply students in grades six and up with index cards for collecting facts, quotes, and ideas. A separate card is used for each piece of information. A good idea is to have cues on the cards (Figure 3.3).

Cards can be color-coded, placed in separate envelopes according to subtopics and questions, and can be reorganized if categories change. Cards allow the students to "play" with the information and organize it to fit their reporting objectives.

During this step of the process, teachers should have their eyes and ears open for student concerns, problems, and questions, and intervene with minilessons in response to specific problems related to reading, evaluating, and organizing information into authentic inquiry products. (Detailed explanations and examples of vocabulary and comprehension minilessons are described in Chapter 8 of this text.) Direct instruction minilessons that are useful in this step of the inquiry project include the concept of definition, semantic maps, self-collection vocabulary cards, question–answer relationships, and how to summarize text. The minilessons on semantic maps and expository mapping in Chapter 8 are especially useful for the next step in the process, evaluating and organizing information.

 Evaluating and Organizing Data

Before we get into the "how to" of evaluating and organizing information, I want to pause and consider the word *information*. This may seem pedantic, but there is confusion because we use concepts like data, information, and knowledge

Information I May Want To Use	
The Fact in my own words:	
The "quote" if I need it:	
Title:	
Author:	**Publisher:**
Page #:	**Year:**

FIGURE 3.3

interchangeably, as I do in this text. But, strictly speaking, these terms are not synonymous. When we are helping students evaluate and organize their notes it makes sense to consider Drucker's observation (1988, p. 49) that raw notes are "data" that only becomes "information" when it is "endowed with relevance and purpose by someone." This means that not all data has the same value, worth, or usefulness. This is why we often have to discard some data, keep other data, and see the need to collect more. To help students transform the raw data they've collected into useful information, teach them to ask questions like:

- Do I have too little, enough, or too much data?
- Did I meet my objectives, answer my questions?
- Is there a way to organize the data with a flow chart, an outline, or another graphic organizer?
- How shall I organize what I've found so it makes sense to me and my audience?

In order to turn data like facts, opinions, and observations into information that satisfies, is useful, and has some purpose, students must evaluate, organize, connect, and retain ideas. Formats for doing this include listing and outlining, and webbing and mapping.

I have found that in research project activities it is wise to use informal organizing. While there is a need to understand formal outlining, trying to impose order with alphabetized and numbered labels with strict spacing rules places "form" ahead of "function" and short-circuits the research process. The goal of organizing is not to create visually correct final outlines as products. Instead, the goal is to "play" with the items and arrange them in ways that make sense. In fact, making lists of items seems to be a natural organizing tool.

Listing. I observed pure list-making when I saw Jeff, a three-year-old, spelling lists of words on a computer. His lists included the typical environmental print he encountered like road signs and street names, as well as words for weather like *rain, wind, storm, lightning,* and *thunder.* At home he did it on his Dad's laptop computer and, when he came to visit me, he often would ask if he could "write some words" on my computer. I also observed that he preferred to write vertical listings of words over writing across a field. Even when I urged him to write his Mom and Dad a note he would say, "no," and continue to make his lists. He preferred listing words and making signs to writing sentences for over two years. I am convinced that letting young children make lists and signs is an overlooked early literacy task. Jeff's list-making reminded me of an experienced special education teacher who used listing to show her students that they were learning. On Fridays she would ask them to list what they had learned that week and the children would make lists of ten to twenty topics they had studied. But, if she asked them to write complete sentences, they would only produce a few. The lists contained more information than sentences and her students were motivated. Both she and I are convinced that their lists were a better indicator of what her students had learned.

Teachers can model making lists and require students to make simple lists of ideas gleaned from reading and listening. Teachers can also model how to arrange the items in some ordered pattern such as levels of importance, time sequence, or clusters of items with similar features. Here is a recent example of how listing worked for three sixth-grade girls who were participating in a thematic study of famous people. Their subtopic focus was famous women scientists. One book they found had a time line containing only two women out of seventy-five famous scientists and inventors, but other books detailed the careers of over fifty women who had made significant contributions. The disparity between sources spurred them to try to find as many women as possible. For their research the girls made a card for each woman scientist or inventor that contained the name, date, and a brief description of her work, scientific activity, or product she produced. At first they tried to organize the names by science areas like chemistry, physics, biology, or commercial products. But as they located more names these categories didn't work very well. And, as they read about the difficulties the women encountered trying to be accepted in the male world of science, they went back and "fixed" the original time line that had omitted women. Here is a portion of the new list they produced, a time line of famous women inventors and scientists:

1871	Martha Coston	Patented Naval Signal Flares
1893	Florence Bascom	Geologist—First Woman PhD in Petrology
1896	Fannie Farmer	Published First Scientific Cookbook
1918	Madam C. F. Walker	First Black American Millionaire Businesswoman
1921	Ida H. Hyde	Physiologist—Developed First Microlectrode
1934	Ruth Benedict	Anthropologist—First Books on Culture and Personality
1947	Gerti Cori	Biochemist—Nobel Prize in Physiology
1952	Grace Hopper	Invented COBOL Computer Language
1957	Bette Nesmith Graham	Invented Liquid Paper Correction Fluid
1960	Jane Goodall	Ethnologist—First to Study Chimpanzees in the Wild
1963	Valentina Tershkova	Soviet Cosmonaut—First Woman in Space
1969	Dorothy Hodgkin	Chemist—Nobel Prize in X-Ray Crystallography
1971	Stephanie Kwolek	Chemist—Invented Kevlar
1983	Barbara McClintock	Nobel Prize in Genetics

1983	Sally Ride	Astrophysicist—First Woman U.S. Astronaut
1984	Judith Resnick	Electrical Engineer—Killed in Challenger Disaster
1984	Christa McAuliffe	Science Teacher—Killed in Challenger Disaster
1996	Shannon Lucid	Biochemist—Longest Time in Space of Any American Astronaut, Aboard Russian Mir Station

Idea Mapping.   Arranging information around questions and concepts is a sure way to make sense out of separate pieces of data. Idea mapping encourages students to link new information around their concerns and their prior knowledge. For example, when the girls in the previous example were looking for famous women scientists and inventors, they found books that described how the women encountered different barriers and difficulties (Stille, 1995; Vare & Ptacek, 1993). To make sense out of this data they mapped names by kinds of difficulties. This array helped them collect and retrieve ideas so they could write sentences like: Women scientists have encountered common problems like not being allowed to study science in colleges and universities, not finding jobs as researchers, not getting credit for their discoveries, and being fired for making new products.

Visual Arrays.   In Chapter 8 there is a minilesson that illustrates how students organize their sources and research notes to fit their questions. Another excellent source for examples of visual strategies that promote active learning is the monograph *Graphic Organizers* (Bromley, Irwin-DeVitis, & Modlo, 1995). It includes straightforward treatments of how teachers and students arrange notes and ideas. Some sample patterns from pages 119–120 are shown in Figure 3.5.

Colleges Resist Women in Science	**No Job as Researchers, Scientists**
• Geology not allowed at Bryn Mawr	• Gerty Cori could only "assist"
• Ida Hyde not allowed to take entrance exams	• Ruth Benedict could only lecture

Difficulties of Women Scientists / Inventors

Not Given Credit	**Fired From Job**
• Rosalind Franklin –no credit for DNA	• Bette Naismith fired from IBM for inventing and selling White-Out

FIGURE 3.4

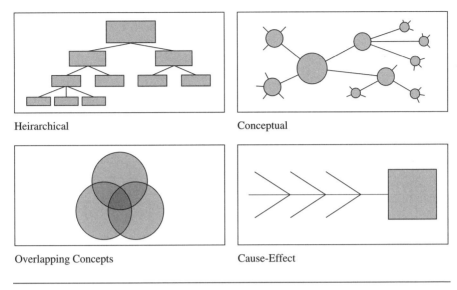

Heirarchical

Conceptual

Overlapping Concepts

Cause-Effect

FIGURE 3.5

These arrays are a good way to visualize ways to describe, think about, and reach conclusions. For example, when students studied famous women scientists and inventors the overlapping concepts array illustrated how women who made widely different contributions shared the overlapping problems of rejection, nonacceptance, anonymity, and lack of recognition.

 **Formats for Reporting**

In the vignette that opened this chapter, Grace wrote a prize-winning fictional story based on the true story of code breaking in World War II. Her writing skill, her teacher's guidance, and the writing contest sponsored by the local reading council prompted her choice of a writing format. While not all sharing and reporting of applied literacy projects will be part of a contest in which students can win prizes, it is good to remember the payoff that comes from having students display a product or perform for an audience.

There are several different formats students can consider as they look ahead and decide how they can best communicate what they have learned. Selection of format is related to purpose. For example, at one school a group of students reported directly to the board of education on their environmental study of water consumption in the school bathrooms. Their inquiry project involved measuring how much water was used by the automatic flushing system that ran for twenty-four hours. The students compared automatic flushing consumption in the boys' bathrooms with use flushing consumption in the girls' bathrooms. They compiled their data and delivered their report directly to the board, claiming that use flushing would save approximately $800 a year. Their choice of a technical report format was dictated by the reality and direct application of their inquiry to the elected officials.

Performance and audience are other factors to consider when selecting a format for sharing and reporting. Just as musicians are motivated to practice by the goal of performance, students are motivated to produce quality inquiry projects when they know their product will be performed in front of an audience, read by the community, or listened to by someone other than their classmates. The table below illustrates a few of the formats to consider.

Writing	*Art*	*Performance*
Advice	Picture Books	Rap and Singing
Column	Posters	Plays
Poetry	Displays	Role Playing
Advertisement	Photographs/Captions	Video or Audio
News Story		

Betsy Brown, a social studies teacher at Lincoln Middle School in Carbondale, Illinois, directed a recent example of a performance format I watched. Four eighth-grade students, Cedar, Laura, Cara, and Lizzie dramatized the Civil War history topic, *Unsung Women of the Civil War.* Betsy approached the girls and told them that the project entailed dramatizing a topic in history of their choosing. The only limit was that the topic had to be related to the theme "Turning Points in History" because that was the National History Day topic for the school history fair. She told them it would entail research, writing a paper, writing a script, and lots of work during their own time. She also pointed out that they would be performing before judges at the regional competition, and that, if they won at that level, they would go on to the state competition in Springfield, Illinois. The winner of the state competition would then go on to compete in Washington, D.C. Betsy said, "They were good students, but not part of the Academically Talented Program. I chose them because they had worked well together in class in the past." The performance project began in November, 1999, and culminated in the performance in April, 2000. Here is a chronology of the inquiry project in Betsy's own words.

> The first order of business was to choose a topic. This required some brainstorming as everyone needed to feel ownership in the topic. We were beginning to study the Civil War at school and Cara and Laura were in favor of a topic in that direction. One deciding factor was that, in order to win and move on to state competition, the project had to relate to Illinois history. I had prior experience with projects dealing with World War II, in which the tie to Illinois was vague, and the project had lost points for this. I

did point out that the Civil War was fought in our backyard, and there would be a lot of local history. With this in mind, the group decided to focus on the Civil War, as that war did have such a huge effect on our history. Now that they had elected to concentrate on the Civil War, a specific topic had to be decided on. I told the group to go and do some research to find out what would be considered a turning point in history. We had another brainstorming meeting, and they decided that the role of women in the war was underplayed and needed telling

One of the first resources to be used was the Internet. Under the topic "Women in the Civil War," the students were introduced to many different women and their accomplishments. They made a list of women who made different contributions, and they narrowed their search to the Sisters of Mercy, Sallie Logan, Jennie Hodgers a.k.a. Albert Cashier, and Mary Bickerdyke. It was now December and time for Christmas break.

In January and early February, the group met once a week after school and, by early February, the group had managed to identify the final group of women who had made contributions and for whom the war was a turning point. Cedar focused her research on Mary Bickerdyke. Lizzie thoroughly researched Jennie Hodgers, who spent fifty years of her life as a man and fought in the war for three years. Laura, however, was disappointed that the Sisters of Mercy had not responded to her December E-mail. At the same time, another woman, named Mary Livermore, kept popping up in the research as someone who was involved in unique ways so Laura's focus became Mary Livermore. Cara read about Mary Logan, and Mary became her focus.

The next step was to find ways to integrate these women and their accomplishments into a script. After careful research, the girls discovered that Mary Bickerdyke and Jennie Hodgers a.k.a. Albert Cashier were actually at the same battle! This was the most exciting discovery and provided the idea for the script. I had secured a videotape of the National History Day winners from 1995 and showed it to the girls, so they would have an idea how a finished script might sound and look. It was really beneficial in sending home the idea that the presentation was a combination of a narrative and vignettes acted out by the participants.

By mid-February the group was meeting several times a week. They decided they wanted to start the script off with each member giving a quote about women and the Civil War. They found a letter Abigail Adams had written to her husband about including women in the Declaration of Independence. They liked how the issue of women's rights was mentioned so long ago and drew the association between how Abigail wanted her husband to remember women just like the accomplishments of women in the Civil War need to be remembered. The title of their project, "Remember the Ladies,'' is actually what Abigail wrote to her husband.

In March the students met three times at my house and twice on their own during that week to memorize the script. I provided them with pizza and chocolate chip cookies to keep the energy flowing! On the last day of spring break I videotaped them running through the script so they could analyze what they needed to improve.

I called in another teacher, Pat Searcy, who had taught drama, and I asked her to evaluate the girls' performance. Each girl dressed in authentic costumes. Lizzie had contacted a local man who is heavily involved with Civil War reenactments, and he provided her with information and a Union uniform. Cara and Cedar obtained patterns of dresses from the Civil War era and had their dresses made. Laura's costuming was more difficult as she had to portray several different characters, both male and female, in the script. We decided on a combination of black pants, a black elastic waist skirt, and a white shirt. The costume was accented with various props—a stethoscope when she was a doctor, a lace cap for her hair and an apron when she was a nurse.

The week before the performance was hectic and, on Friday before the Saturday morning performance, we worked well into the evening. The girls went home singing at 10 P.M., pleased with their final product. The next day they performed for the judges at the History Fair. Although the group did not go on to perform at the state contest in Springfield, they did get an excellent rating. Overall they said they learned interesting history, and enjoyed the work, and got a lot out of the project. Their parents echoed those sentiments as well.

 Evaluating Inquiry Products

Perhaps more than ever before educational accountability plays a significant role in the lives of teachers. To demonstrate this I have placed evaluation up front in the next, not the last, chapter of this book. And, while it's true that educational standards and mandated testing of students are at the forefront of school improvement efforts, the applied literacy products and performances of students are, in my estimation, superior sources of evidence for demonstrating student achievement. For instance, what is more powerful evidence of ongoing achievement, a score on a high-stakes, one-time test or an authentic applied literacy activity that engaged students for several weeks? Test scores do count, of course, but they pale in comparison to sustained student performances that illustrate how literacy skills are used and new information is applied and communicated.

One way to deal with the evaluation of inquiry activities is to use the traditional process and product distinctions. The process evaluation idea means that evaluation focuses on the inquiry process itself while the product evaluation focuses on the product and/or performance end.

Process Questions and Sources of Evidence.   Ongoing inquiry is evaluated with questions like: Does inquiry make sense to students? Is it working? Do students value the process? Are they engaged and actively involved? What do students' attitudes reveal? Are there enough sources to support inquiry? What steps seem to be the easiest or the hardest? Where do students need the most help?

Artifacts produced during inquiry are excellent kinds of evidence for illustrating the extent to which students understand, use, and value the inquiry process. Teachers report that it is a good idea to supply students with a booklet in which they keep a log of their progress. Another organization plan is to supply students with file folders, notebooks, and formats for keeping track of evidence. Some teachers have students keep an anecdotal journal in which they record their progress, problems, and concerns on a weekly basis. Teachers also keep their own anecdotal journals to keep track of what students are experiencing. Keeping track of students prompts the teacher to know when to intervene, when to get out of the way, and how to improve the use of the inquiry process.

Product Questions and Sources of Evidence.   When we look for a payoff at the end, we ask questions like: Did the report answer the questions? Was the final product clear, meaningful, and useful? Did the performance communicate ideas and information clearly to the audience? What did the audience say about the report, the performance? Did the final product meet or exceed local and state educational goals and outcomes?

In addition to grading quizzes, tests, written products, and performances, teachers and students use checklists and rubrics to document student learning. In the next chapter and in the appendix there is an extensive description of actual checklists and rubrics that teachers and students are using to evaluate their efforts and products. There is also a detailed example of how to tie student outcomes to state educational standards.

Summary

This chapter described the following seven steps that you can use as a format to guide students in applied literacy activities:

Selecting topics and themes
Raising issues and questions
Inquiry planning: Search strategies and data sources
Reading, listening, selecting, and recording data
Evaluating and organizing data
Reporting formats
Evaluating inquiry products

These steps are neither a sacred ritual that has to be unthinkingly followed nor are they simple suggestions that can be easily overlooked with no consequences. They are guidelines for planning and implementing an exciting way to teach. My rule of thumb is that teachers always have to adapt and improvise if they want to connect with their students. The uncertainty and variance in teaching styles, materials, student interests, and student skills that exist in every classroom and school dictates adaptation. If you try to follow the steps to the letter you may find yourself stymied by the rigidity. If you skip some steps or treat some too lightly, problems can arise that will confuse students. You will have to style the inquiry process to fit the particular situation dictated by your students, your grade level, the resources you have on hand, and your own way of motivating and directing students. One piece of advice is to not be afraid of making mistakes implementing the inquiry process with novice researchers. Learn from them and trust your own and your students' curiosity. A final tip is that you will always need to use minilessons and other scaffolding ideas to increase the chances that students, as rookie researchers, will experience success.

Recently, a fourth-grade teacher described the promises and perils of using inquiry, and I end this chapter with her optimism and honesty.

> I am at the beginning of an exciting journey into science inquiry with my students . . . As their teacher, my role will be to guide them through the complicated inquiry process . . . I will make more colossal mistakes, but I will learn from them . . . My mistakes mark the risks I am taking and allow me to ask the questions that lead me in new directions with my teaching and learning (Tower, 2000, p. 556).

References

Bromley, K., Irwin-De Vitis, L., & Modlo, M. (1995). *Graphic organizers: Visual strategies for active learning.* New York: Scholastic.

Cherry, L. (1997). *Flute's journey: The life of a wood thrush.* New York: Trumpet.

Crosswhite, L. (1999). *More ideas for using nonfiction effectively in your classroom.* Danbury, CT: Grolier.

Drucker, P. F. (1988, January/February). The coming of the new organization. *Harvard Business Review, 66,* 45–53.

Kobrin, D. (1992). *In there with the kids.* Boston: Houghton Mifflin.

Ogle, D. (1986). K-W-L: A teaching model that develops active reading of expository text. *Reading Teacher, 39,* 564–570.

Sickler, L. (2000, March 13). The write stuff. *The Southern Illinoisan,* Vol. 108, pp. 2A+.

Stille, D. R. (1995). *Extraordinary women scientists.* Chicago: Children's Press.

Tower, C. (2000). Questions that matter: Preparing elementary students for the inquiry process. *Reading Teacher, 53*(7), 550–557.

Vare, E. A., & Ptacek, M. (1993). *Women inventors and their discoveries.* Minneapolis: Oliver Press.

4

Student Engagement and Learning Outcomes

I love it when my students find information from different sources and read, respond, argue, decide, believe, and act.

Ann, Seventh-Grade Teacher

In this chapter student motivation and teacher accountability for applied literacy activities are discussed. For classroom teachers these two concerns are the top criteria for judging the credibility of any teaching idea. Teachers want to know whether or not students cared about a book, a lesson, or a particular activity because a powerful source of teacher satisfaction is when students are eager, engaged, and learning. Student response is a very personal *inside* kind of evaluation that all teachers do when they consider the value of a teaching idea. Therefore, the first part of this chapter describes how applied literacy activities engage students.

The second part of the chapter addresses the issue of accountability. Teachers know they have to demonstrate that their lessons have some payoff for meeting district and state educational goals and outcomes. This is a powerful *outside* kind of evaluation that teachers do because they know they are being watched closely today. Therefore, the second part of the chapter describes how teachers link applied literacy activities to district and state learning outcomes.

These two concerns mark both sides of the territory teachers occupy in the schema of education. Teachers feel accountable to both their students and to the larger community. This chapter provides evidence that applied literacy activities cover both the inside issue of engaging students and the outside issue of accountability.

Vignette: Applied Literacy Is Engaging

Sixth-grade teacher, Matt, initiated the unit on Castles by starting with a protective habitat that was familiar to his students—their homes. He wrote on the chalkboard, What things in our homes protect us?, and asked the whole class for responses. The students started with obvious items like locks, smoke alarms, and fire extinguishers. But, with some prompting from Matt, they quickly listed over thirty things. Next, he helped the class organize the items into categories: safety concerns, homes today, and castles in the past. When they were done they had the following compare/contrast array.

How do habitats protect people?

Concerns	In Our Homes Today	In Castles in the Past
Food/Water	Water filters, stoves, refrigerators, pantries	
Weather	Roof, windows, furnaces, air conditioning, basement shelters (tornadoes), strong construction (hurricanes)	
Pests/Insects	Screens, poisons, traps, barriers, exterminators, cats	
Fire	Smoke alarms, fire extinguishers, 911, safety rules	
Crime/Enemies	Locks, lights, alarms, police, neighborhood watch, guns, fences, watchdog	
Pollution/Poisons	Filters, carbon monoxide detectors, safe, containers, locked storage spaces, plumbing, toilets	
Noise/Privacy	Insulation, trees, fences, window shades, shrubs	

The array was the basis for a whole-class discussion on why and how people build protective habitats. The discussion led to questions and Matt modeled how the array prompted him to think about the past. He modeled this by asking the class, "I wonder if people in the past had the same concerns we have today for protection from dangers like pollution and crime?" The discussion that followed covered a broad range of student concerns from fires and tornadoes to burglars and rotten food. The students were sharing experiences and asking questions when Matt asked, "Do you think people living in castles had the same concerns for safety and comfort that we have today?" Some students said no, others said yes and Matt had to call out names to stop the loud and heated arguing. When it calmed down he said, "Some concerns are the same today, like the need for good food and water, fear of fire, fear of bad weather. Others might be different. Is our fear of enemies and crime today different than the fear of enemies that people living in castles had in the past?" This prompted a lively discussion comparing how we protect ourselves today from crime, war, and violence and how people might have protected themselves when they lived in castles.

At this point the students began to ask questions and Matt began making a list of questions about life in castles. These questions were saved and reproduced on several large sheets of easel paper. Matt planned to have teams of students select questions and read from a variety of sources to try to answer the questions they were most interested in. Matt was pleased when Maggie, Zack, and Kurt decided to find out if castles had bathrooms and plumbing, while Alicia, Jerry, and Nell decided to find out what people did for food and entertainment inside the castle. He thought the study of castles was off to a good start. He hoped the initial interest would sustain the students through the process of seeking information, evaluating and organizing information, and using the information to present reports on not only castles but also some of the features of all protective habitats.

This vignette illustrates how a teacher uses a compare-and-contrast format that engages his students to ask questions. Student questions are a source of energy that Matt skillfully taps. He knows that they are necessary if he wants his class to search for information from a variety of sources. We know that even the best materials and methods will not guarantee learning. Students must care and place some value on what they are attempting to learn. Matt will supply some questions, but he knows that better thinking and learning occur when he guides students to ask their own questions. In the next section recent research on literacy learning and motivation is reviewed to substantiate how Matt employed his students' knowledge of modern home safety to help them raise questions about the past lives of people living in castles.

A Motivation Equation: Challenges, Chums, and Choices

The literature on student engagement and motivation can help us understand why Matt's class is off to a good start on their inquiry project. When students are *challenged* but not overwhelmed, when they are allowed to collaborate with their *chums,* and when they have some autonomy or *choices* about what to learn and what strategies to use to try to learn, they are more motivated to read and write (Turner, 1997). Matt's planned discussion on homes and castles motivated his students because he started with what the students already know about their homes as protective habitats. He showed them that they can start with what they already know and apply that to a new domain. When tasks appear challenging, but doable, students feel as though they are making self-improvement rather than just doing what the teacher tells them to do. They also use more learning strategies and often seek help from others. For this reason Matt wants them to work in teams that can select questions they wish to answer. Choice of topics and questions to do research about increases the chances that different student interests will be addressed, such as the boys' interests in castle plumbing and the girls' interests in food and entertainment. Matt is attempting to create a classroom where student choices about topics, sources, teammates, strategies, and products increases responsibility and fosters confidence and independence.

While Matt is off to a good start, he is far from turning students loose to find answers to their questions. He will have to scaffold a host of other applied literacy tasks that are described in subsequent chapters of this text. The truth is that middle-grade students are novices who need guidance and encouragement throughout the entire journey from asking questions to preparing reports. The journey from questions to answers takes time and the next section describes how teachers integrate their curriculum to provide for richer learning time.

Integrating Content and Literacy Lessons Is Motivating

In addition to creating thematic lessons that feature challenges, choices, and chums, Matt's protective habitat unit on castles integrates reading and language arts with history and social studies. This is a formidable task. There is always uncertainty in teaching. Shouldn't Matt play it safe and cover all of the content in the social studies text? Matt, like more and more teachers, has decided that he needs to cover less content and provide students with "rich, in-depth studies relying primarily on hands-on activities, library materials and both fiction and non-fiction books" (Santa, 1997, pp. 228–229). Matt is not alone today in his belief that selecting sources, reading, note taking, researching and writing reports, and making oral presentations in the castle study means he does need a separate time for language arts. Students will be learning and using language arts strategies as they carry out their research and share their results, but how does he know his students are learning both content information and literacy strategies? What evidence can he use to show to parents, school officials, and the community that integrating the language arts and content areas and providing in-depth studies pays off? The next section describes what teachers do to tie applied literacy lessons to educational standards and goals.

Accountability with Rubrics, Checklists, and Portfolios

That classroom teaching is marked by high uncertainty is not a revelation, but teachers work under unprecedented pressures and criticism in America today. Standardized testing is on the rise and one response is to spend school time teaching students to pass a specific high-stakes test. Another response is to seek teaching methods that will raise test scores. At workshops I conduct on applied literacy teachers ask, "Will these materials and methods raise the test scores?" One middle-school teacher told me, "My superintendent sent me to this workshop to find ways to improve our state test scores." The pressure for high test scores goes beyond the classroom: in some districts parents have refused to let their children be tested, and in other schools students, teachers, and school officials have cheated to inflate scores. Perhaps the most sinister outcome of high-stakes testing is when test content and test performance become the curriculum. This "dumbing down" of the curriculum is just the opposite of what all the surveillance is supposed to do—improve schools. Teachers know that one-shot tests are only snapshots so they respond with real-life documentary evaluation devices.

I continually meet teachers who, instead of moving to a simple-minded test-taking curriculum, rally together to create some powerful tools for documenting student growth and achievement in literacy skills, critical thinking strategies, and content information. The following rubrics and student portfolios illustrate how resilient teachers are when challenged to defend practices they believe in.

Student-Centered Literacy Rubrics

Teachers in Colorado (Guy, 2001; Guy & Wasserstein, 1996) report that they use reading, writing, speaking, and listening rubrics with their students to assess growth and to show how students are meeting Colorado's learning standards. The teachers developed a unit in which children do research on "Birds of Prey." As the children search for information, read sources, take notes, draft reports, and prepare written documents, the teachers and students use rubrics and checklists. When students give oral reports and listen to other student reports, the teachers and students use checklists and rubrics to assess growth in speaking and listening.

The entire set of rubric items is found in Appendix A. Later, in Chapter 9 of this book, I describe the "Birds of Prey" unit in more detail to show the teaching materials and the management steps the teachers followed for the nine-week unit. For now, notice how the following rubric items for writing are written in the first person and are easy to understand. Students and teachers use the items and the summary sheet to fix drafts and make changes that improve the final reports.

Writing

Ideas and Content	4	3	2	1
Organization	4	3	2	1
Voice	4	3	2	1
Word Choice	4	3	2	1
Sentence Structure	4	3	2	1
Writing Conventions	4	3	2	1

Ideas and Content

4 • My writing skillfully meets the requirements of the task and is interesting to the reader.

 • I show that I know my topic well and express ideas that are interesting and unique. I write thoughtfully about my ideas and weave them together to improve meaning.

- I stick to my topic and clearly communicate important ideas, carefully choosing details that make my subject clear and interesting.
3 - My writing meets the requirements of the task and is interesting to the reader.
- I show that I know my topic well and communicate my ideas to the reader.
- I stick to my topic. I have enough details to make the topic clear and keep the reader interested.
2 - My writing makes sense, but I did not meet all of the requirements of the task.
- I know my topic, but I need to include more information in my writing.
- I may have spent too much time on information that was not important or not enough time on important ideas.
1 - My main idea was not clear, and I did not meet the requirements of the task.
- I need more information about my topic.
- I did not stick to my topic, or I did not have much to say.

Portfolios

When students and teachers combine drafts, notes, and reports with rubrics and checklists, they create portfolios. Portfolios are a popular and effective way to assess authentic inquiry and they place the responsibility and control for assessment in the hands of teachers and students (Farr & Tone, 1994; Valencia, 1990). Working portfolios are folders, files, notebooks, and places where student notes, drafts, and documents are placed to demonstrate how students are managing the inquiry process. Show portfolios contain final products like written reports, audiovisual reports, posters, and other material that students create in order to communicate with others. Along with the student products, portfolios contain checklists and rubrics that summarize and evaluate both the processes and products.

For example, the Colorado teachers and students have working and show portfolios and use the reading, writing, speaking, and listening rubrics to assess both the drafts and the final products. Teachers and students review working portfolios together during the unit to help manage the research process. Final reports and rubrics are the raw data that show how students are meeting Colorado standards in reading and language arts. The Colorado teachers say that portfolios and rubrics are the best way to assess authentic inquiry because students get continuous feedback. They see what they need to change and they know when they have been successful. The teachers also have evidence to show how they and their students are accountable to the Colorado learning standards.

Portfolios are usually worked with on a weekly, not a daily basis. Teachers also conference with students by going through the portfolio together on a bi- or tri-weekly basis. If students work in teams, group portfolios work well and are the focus of conferences. Teachers try to conference with all students or groups on a weekly or bi-weekly rotating basis.

Some cautions to observe with portfolios (Reutzel & Cooter, 2000) include keeping too much student work, spending too much time managing portfolios, and making too many teacher entries. One way teachers and students deal with bulky portfolios is to cull material after a conference. Some material can be sent home to be saved while other material may be noted on the rubrics and checklists and then destroyed. One way teachers deal with time pressure is to limit portfolio management time to one thirty- to forty-five-minute session per week. And teachers do not write reviews on everything. Instead, students select one or two pieces for the teacher to comment on, or teachers select the sample when they decide it is important to review the work. The trick is to remember that portfolios are not the goal. They are a tool for assessing progress, giving feedback, and documenting student achievement with authentic artifacts.

Learning Outcomes Matched to Educational Goals

Another approach to assessment and accountability is to key student literacy outcomes to state and/or national learning standards. In Illinois, at a 1997 school district Goals 2000 summer workshop on critical thinking, teachers planned thematic units and keyed students' performance and products to the state learning standard number five that says students will use language arts to acquire, assess, and communicate information (Carbondale Elementary District #95, 1997). To assess how students used critical thinking, the teachers made a list of critical thinking outcomes and matched them to thematic unit learning activities. Student activities and products were collected in portfolios and the list of outcomes served as a checklist. The teachers prefaced their critical thinking lessons with the following philosophy statement that integrates language arts and critical thinking. Notice how their philosophy is based on several beliefs about critical thinking and literacy, students as future citizens, and the role of teachers.

Critical Thinking and Literacy

Philosophy:
We believe it is essential that we equip our students with skills that enable them to think critically and engage in problem solving. In a world where a flood of information bombards people, the ability to critically evaluate information is crucial. We believe we can help our students by conducting language arts learning activities that teach critical thinking.

Critical thinking involves reflective thought that is focused on what we believe or disbelieve and what to do or not to do. Underlying critical thinking is the tendency

(continued)

or disposition to do the following: ask relevant questions, seek reasons, look for a thesis, use credible sources, look at the big picture, stick to the main point, keep the basic concern in mind, look for alternatives, and be open-minded. In addition, we believe critical thinking enables individuals to take (and change) an informed position on an issue in the face of sufficient evidence. Finally, we believe critical thinking also enables individuals to be sensitive to the position others take on issues.

We believe a fully literate person has the ability to analyze arguments, ask and answer questions that challenge and clarify, judge source credibility, make deductions, infer from single and multiple sources, make value judgments, define terms, decide on actions, and interact confidently with others.

Students As Future Citizens in a Democracy.

As we prepare students to be productive citizens living in a democratic society we realize that the language arts lessons we deliver provide an ideal situation to teach critical thinking. Productive and effective citizens are informed by reading and listening and they communicate clearly and effectively by speaking and writing. Because a democracy requires constant care we believe that an emphasis on critical thinking while reading, writing, speaking and listening is crucial to preparing students to live and work together in a cooperative spirit of tolerance and fair play.

Teaching Critical Thinking in Language Arts.

We believe critical thinking is best learned when students are active and engaged learners who participate, explore, and create information. We believe this occurs when students encounter information organized around meaningful themes and concepts. We believe students learn best when they take pride in and apply their knowledge to new situations. We believe that the skills underlying critical thinking are best learned when they are integrated into language arts learning activities.

Goals and Standards.

The learning activities and outcomes for critical thinking are related to the English language arts goals established by the Illinois State Board of Education (1997). In addition to the four broad state goals for reading, writing, speaking, and listening, the learning activities in this guide focus on Goal Five and standards related to acquiring, assessing, and communicating information.

Goal Five:

Students will use the language arts to acquire, assess, and communicate information.

Learning Standards:

A. Students will locate, organize, and use information from various sources to answer questions, solve problems, communicate ideas. (ACQUIRE)
B. Students will analyze and evaluate information acquired from various sources. (ASSESS)
C. Students will apply acquired information, concepts, and ideas to communicate in a variety of formats. (COMMUNICATE)

Critical Thinking Outcomes.
In the following unit of study the students use a multitude of critical thinking behaviors to ACQUIRE, ASSESS, and COMMUNICATE information. The critical thinking behaviors embedded in the following unit are identified by the abbreviated codes. For example, when students discuss why ads are appealing and when they identify specific propaganda techniques they are coded DC and RFD to show that students could draw conclusions and read for details. Copies of this checklist are placed in the portfolios and teachers and students mark the critical thinking outcomes that appear in the artifacts on display.

Acquire

FD	Read and locate detailed information
Rc	Listen and recall a specific idea or word
Sum	Summarize
BR	Brainstorm
P	Paraphrase
In	Infer
DC	Draw Conclusions
Main	Identify Main Ideas

Assess

C&C	Generate a Compare and Contrast List
S&D	Same and Different
SCL	Sort and Classify information
C-F	Determine Cause and Effect
TOP	Identify Text Organization Patterns Persuasive
TON	Identify Text Organization Patterns Narrative
TOEx	Identify Text Organization Patterns Expository
JC	Judge Credibility of a Source
ACT	Analyze Character Traits
Th	Identify Themes
PV	Identify Point of View
FL	Identify figurative language

Communicate

WJ	Write in journal
WR	Write informational report
AuS	Author a story
TS	Tell story
Dem	Demonstrate a skill
PR	Present report
IntD	Interpret data
VidAud	Make video/audio of story or report
WP	Write poetry
Deb	Participate in debate
IL	Illustrate report or story
Wcp	Write captions
Grp	Make graph

Sample Learning Activity

In the following example, Carbondale teachers created a unit on propoganda techniques found in advertising. To show that their students used critical thinking to recognize propoganda, coded behaviors were matched to teaching activities. This allows them to demonstrate how their students are meeting state reading and language arts goal number five.

Theme: Making Sense of Citizenship   **Learning Activity:** Persuasive Savvy
Grade: Seventh-Grade Social Studies—Language Arts
Outcome: Students will identify and use persuasive techniques
Materials/Resources: Propaganda handout, TV commercials, advertising copy from media

Procedure:
Acquire

DC   1. Watch two video commercials that appeal to youth and discuss why they like or dislike the product.
RFD 2. Explain propaganda techniques: transfer of feelings, testimonial, plain folks appeal, bandwagon, glittering generalization, impressive language, discrediting, euphemism.

Assess

JC   1. Examine persuasive ads, editorials for persuasive techniques.

Communicate

IntD 1. Student teams of 2–3 members collect examples of persuasive ads and other material and try to find at least five kinds of propaganda.
WIR 2. Teams make scrapbooks of ads with persuasive techniques clearly identified. Scrapbooks are shared with brief oral descriptions and put on display at parent open house.

One team of middle-grade teachers made a matrix of all the acquire, assess, communicate outcomes they had generated for their thematic lessons and they found plenty of acquire and communicate outcomes. The lack of assess outcomes led them to add activities that helped novice researchers judge the reliability and validity of their sources. Teachers said the matrix of outcomes helped them feel confident that they could show how their applied literacy lessons were meeting state reading and language arts standards.

National Standards and Applied Literacy

In addition to state standards, teachers find support for applied literacy in the *Standards for the English Language Arts* developed by the National Council of

Teachers of English and the International Reading Association (1996). The twelve standards are found in Appendix B. Notice how closely authentic inquiry matches standard seven:

> Students conduct research on issues and interests by generating ideas and questions, and by posing problems. They gather, evaluate, and synthesize data from a variety of sources (e.g., print and non-print texts, artifacts, people) to communicate their discoveries in ways that suit their purpose and audience (p. 25).

In addition, standards one and eight direct teachers to have students read a wide range of print and nonprint texts and use a variety of technological and informational resources (e.g., libraries, databases, computer networks, video) to gather, synthesize, create, and communicate information. These and other national standards lend support to teachers who must justify their curriculum to their peers, to parents, to boards of education, and to communities.

Summary

I have addressed two important concerns of teachers in this chapter. On a school and classroom basis teachers know the prime importance of motivating students so they search for materials and activities that engage students to raise concerns and questions. On the other hand, teachers know they are accountable so they develop rubrics, checklists, portfolios, and goal-based outcome plans that align teaching activities and student processes and products with district, state, and national learning standards.

References

Carbondale Elementary District #95. (1997). *Goals 2000 grant: Language arts and critical thinking skills.* Carbondale, IL: Author.

Farr, R., & Tone, B. (1994). *Portfolio and performance assessment.* Fort Worth, TX: Harcourt Brace.

Guy, C. L. Personal communication, May 2, 2001.

Guy, C. L., & Wasserstein, P. (1996, February 4). *The marriage of instruction and evaluation.* Paper presented at Colorado Council IRA meeting in Denver.

Illinois State Board of Education. (1997). *Illinois Learning Standards.* Springfield, IL: Author.

Reutzel, D. R., & Cooter, R. B. (2000). *Teaching children to read* (3rd ed.). Upper Saddle River, NJ: Merrill.

Santa, C. (1997). School change and literacy engagement: Preparing teaching and learning environments. In J. Guthrie & A. Wigfield (Eds.), *Reading engagement: Motivating readers through integrated instruction* (pp. 218–233). Newark, DE: International Reading Association.

Standards for the English Language Arts. (1996). Urbana, IL: National Council of Teachers of English, and Newark DE: International Reading Association.

Turner, J. C. (1997). Strategies for engaging young literacy learners. In J. Guthrie & A. Wigfield (Eds.), *Reading engagement: Motivating readers through integrated instruction* (pp. 183–204). Newark, DE: International Reading Association.

Valencia, S. (1990). A portfolio approach to classroom reading assessment: The whys, whats, and hows. *Reading Teacher, 43*(4), 338–340.

5

Real-World Connections: New Time and Space, New Roles, and New Community Relationships

Little has changed in the ways that schools divide time and space.
Tyrack & Cuban, 1995

Applied literacy activities lead children to learning that is connected directly to the real world in terms of time and space concepts. In addition, authentic inquiry demands new roles for media specialists and parents, and forges new ways to connect school activities to the world of work in the community. When schools implement applied literacy activities, the staff is confronted with new perspectives on school time and changes in classroom space. Authentic inquiry also features expanded roles for school library media specialists, new roles for parents, and new school and workplace connections. In this chapter I present some examples of new time and space concepts, expanded staff and parent roles, as well as an example of how applied literacy connects school and the workplace. The chapter begins with my retelling of events associated with a recent teacher workshop.

Change Threatens Long-Held Beliefs

I was sharing nonfiction materials and ideas on applied literacy activities at a local workshop with elementary and middle-school teachers when the principal asked, "Do you know of any schools we could visit where they have gone all the way with inquiry-based teaching? Seeing how they do it would help because we want to go in this direction." After I told him I was pleased that he was supportive of inquiry I said, "There probably are schools, but I can't name one offhand. My hunch is that individual teachers or small teams of teachers implement applied literacy." We talked for a while, and agreed that visiting other model schools is a good idea, but that we will always have to deal with our own unique school culture and implement applied literacy as a "do-it-yourself" project.

The day following the workshop, national TV news clips showed the latest shuttle launch to bring new parts to the space station. That the current launch was no big deal today prompted me to recall the past when it was a big deal to put people into space. In the early 1960s, in my sixth-grade classroom, we all watched black-and-white TV as John Glenn's space capsule went up and came down in the ocean after a brief orbiting journey. Compared to yesterday's tiny one-man capsule, we now have a reusable shuttle that carries people and cargo to an orbiting space station where people stay for months at a time. Compared to yesterday's classroom where twenty-five students sat in rows in front of me for about 180 days, we now have classrooms where twenty-five students sit in rows with one teacher for just a little more than 180 days. My point is that space technology has changed drastically in forty years while the basic time, space, and learning arrangement for school children is still like my classroom forty years ago. And, just as the old one-man space capsule will not work in today's space program, our long-held time and space practices will not support full-blown applied literacy learning.

The principal in my story is an excellent instructional leader whom I admire and respect, and I believe him when he says the school is moving toward new applied literacy and inquiry learning practices. But when the workshop continued, the teachers' comments and questions revealed that the widespread adoption of applied literacy activities threatened long-held beliefs about classroom time and space. Comments like, "When is there time to go to the computers in the library? We may not have a place for students to present reports. We have little storage place where students can store their materials and projects. There are not enough stations for all students to do in-depth searches on the Internet. Because time is limited, which subjects do we not cover when we do applied literacy?"

Nonlinear Time

Other teachers have faced these authentic concerns, so I will discuss some basic time and space changes that occur when applied literacy activities are implemented. For example, in a later chapter there is a copy of the letter that eighth-grade science teacher, Greg Reid, sends to parents warning that school will be "ill-structured" for the nine-week soil science unit. He is warning parents and students that teaching/learning will not proceed in a linear fashion with predefined activities done in a specific order. Instead of following a sequence controlled by the text and the teacher, the activities are selected and sequenced by teams of students. While all classes are involved in the soil science Heartland Project for the same nine weeks, some students will be doing soil science experiments, others will be researching genetically modified organisms on the Internet, and others will be designing and distributing a survey on peoples' attitudes about organic food products. All of these will be going on simultaneously and the students dictate the sequence and duration based on the activity, not the clock or a text. Of course, the nine-week grading period dictates that teams of students will complete their research and prepare and present a report in time for Greg Reid to assign grades.

This way of conducting school is ill-structured and chaotic in comparison to the expected teacher routines that are ingrained and taken for granted. The point is not that controlling students, following a linear time schedule, teaching prescribed material to groups of varying abilities, and sorting students by high, average, and low achievement are bad practices that must be ended. The point is that school time and space routines are so embedded in the culture that teachers have trouble visualizing how they will get students to learn from multiple information sources, produce original reports, and complete projects that demonstrate learning. Applied literacy activities are ill structured because they lead teachers to experience nonlinear time in new and different-looking classrooms.

Bending and Stretching School Time

In school the clock and calendar rule. Teachers consistently say that the biggest problems they face are the lack of time to prepare lessons and the lack of class time to teach everything in the curriculum. Communities fund expensive remedial programs that, by definition, are linear time-oriented that are supposed to help children who are "behind" to "catchup." There are political and educational leaders who chant that all children must learn to read by third grade and that far too many fourth-grade children are not yet proficient readers. What's the big hurry? I don't think there is any place else in life where a linear or straight-line view of time dominates as much as it does in school.

When we get away from school and look at other settings, time is not always linear. For instance, a teacher friend explained that she and her husband have time conflicts. She says the conflict is because she operates on linear time and fusses when events do not start and stop at predicted times. However, her husband is a civil engineer who has a curved and flexible view of time because construction projects never proceed in a straight line from start to finish. His work projects create their own time. There are always delays and problems that interrupt progress. In his work setting, interruptions are not failures. Instead, time and work interact so that, if some part of the project stops, they work on another part. If the project is slowed seriously by unforeseen events, new deadlines are set. In the construction world the work creates its own time that is curved, circular, adjustable. Happily, the teacher and the engineer have discussed this, and she understands why he does not think it is a problem to delay dinner and he understands why she wants him home to eat dinner at a preset time.

Because school time is straight and rigid, a curved and multidimensioned time experience in the classroom is often first perceived as chaos, a failure. For example, one teacher who implemented a literacy workshop in his seventh-grade language arts class said he came close to being lost when things did not proceed in a linear fashion from book to book and writing to writing. He said, "Time was not that regular rolling of sea to shore, wave after predictable wave; it was something else" (McAndrew, 1993). I believe he discovered that, when students are actively constructing learning, they follow a variety of time orders and sequences much like the construction engineer has to follow. He says his distress was eased when he read about new science concepts about time that claim "events in the world do not occur in a linear or chronological fashion, as a chain of before-now-after tick tock of a clock" (McAndrew, p. 165). Instead, he believes that active literacy time in his class is not chaos "but rather the time of active literacy" (p. 168). Instead of reading and writing being controlled by a linear and highly organized sequence of predetermined teacher and school time, student-controlled reading and writing creates its own kind of circular and active time.

With students studying multiple sources and working in teams to prepare reports, typical linear time conditions give way to circular construction engineering time conditions. Different students and different literacy activities will proceed at different rates and tasks will be competed in different sequences. McAndrew says teachers will see that, with applied literacy:

> the teaching and learning of literacy unfold at their own rate, in their own time . . . as new science would see it, . . . time organically arising from and being defined by reading, writing, learning, and kids. Time was not a lock step of classes and units marching to June (p. 168).

McAndrew's experience with the new time of classroom writing workshop conflicts with the long-held practice of moving students along in lockstep fashion. If you follow state or district policies that specify the number of minutes for each subject, you are only doing what is expected. In this linear time world failure for both students and teachers is when expected learning goals are not met at the specified time. However, when teachers and students are engaged in applied literacy activities they create open blocks of flexible time. This gives them room to bend and stretch time so the students have time to do research, take notes, organize data, and prepare reports.

Flexible Time Examples

In the elementary grades the typical self-contained classroom arrangement enables teachers to combine time allotments to create weekly blocks of time that allow students to pursue learning activities in a "loosely structured" manner. For example, in order to have three or four ninety-minute blocks of inquiry time during each week, teachers combine science, social studies, reading, and language arts times. The longer time periods enable individual students as well as small teams to do different tasks at the same time. So, while some students work with the teacher, others are meeting and editing a part of their project, while others are searching for information. In grades three through five a typical applied literacy project may last three to six weeks, while in grades six through eight projects often last a full nine-week grading period. In middle school a schedule of forty- to sixty-minute periods is often fixed. Some schools are able to combine these into longer blocks by having two or more teachers alter the schedule while others are not able to do this.

However, many educational time schemes have to follow a calendar of school-grading periods. Daily and weekly time arrangements demand flexible time-line planning. In order to meet grade reporting deadlines teachers develop task-oriented checkoff sheets to manage extended projects. During a project, different activities happen at times dictated by the topic, the sources of information, technology availability, and the individual and group choices made by the students and teachers. The teachers build in catch-up times, review times, and create flexible deadlines. The ebb and flow of student-centered learning controls the rate of progress while the beginning and ending are set by the calendar. Here is a sample plan that illustrates how teachers and students negotiate time in order to conduct a research paper project that spans an eight- or nine-week grading period.

Project Topic/Question _____

Name _____ Class/Teacher _____

Week 1   Project letter sent home, meet in learning center, assign text pp. 5–11, view research video, discuss research topics/questions, students select topic/question, learn to make note cards, select one source, make and hand in note card. Student teams organized.

Topic _____
Notes _____

Week 2   Teacher models topic map. Teams map own topics. Select secondary sources books, magazines. Find Internet source, locate primary source for interview. Read text pp. 12–20 on organizing notes

Maps _____
Source lists _____

Week 3   Meet in learning center, solve problems, teams share topic maps, continue to locate information and refine questions. 10–15 note cards due.

Notes _____

Week 4   Continue to collect information, teachers provide help to teams and individuals, teach minilesson on summarizing, review note-card formatting, review interviewing questions. 20 note cards due.

Notes _____

Week 5   Continue collecting information, teachers provide help, model draft of report passed out. Read text pp. 25–35. 30 note cards due. Teach report organization, begin drafts of introduction, body, conclusion.

Notes _____

Week 6   Rough drafts worked on with teacher help. Catch-up week. Last week to gather information. Rough draft due Friday. Rubrics for editing/publishing shared.

Draft copy _____

Week 7   Drafts edited, student editing teams review reports, last week to revise, edit. Reports published, word processing.

Report copy _____

Week 8   Teacher editing and formatting with headings, page numbers, citations. Reporting formats planned. Published and presented, rubrics completed. ____

Week 9   Final papers due.   _____

Reports presented.   _____

Classroom Space: Construction Sites and Studios

There is an engaging photograph of the outside of an old wooden, unpainted and abandoned one-room schoolhouse under high cirrus clouds on the cover of *Foundations of American Education* (Hlebowitsh, 2001). The photograph does not have to show the inside; we all know that there are rows of desks facing a teacher's desk and a chalkboard. And while the text is loaded with information about the past, present, and future of U.S. education, there is not one bit of information in the new book about the past, present, and future of classroom space. I suspect this is so because there has been no need to change. Classrooms continue to be the place where students sit down to listen, read, write, and recite.

But what happens when inquisitive students search multiple sources, collect data, work in teams, construct reports and displays, and make presentations? Classrooms change into construction sites and studios. Tables replace desks, computers replace encyclopedias, and extension cords snake across the floor. Existing classrooms and the new ones under construction today are not much different than the old one-room school—a thirty-by-35-foot space where same-aged students are expected to read, write, listen, and recite in an orderly and quiet fashion. There will be one door opening onto a hallway and one wall will hold a chalkboard. One look at this and you know immediately the space is designed for control of students and teacher-centered lecturing.

As I write this, I am reminded of a story about Frank Lloyd Wright, the famous architect who designed a church in the Midwest. He was asked, "Why are the windows in the Sunday school classrooms way up near the ceiling? No one can look out and view the lake next to the church." He is supposed to have sarcastically said, "The little beggars are not supposed to be looking out the windows during Sunday school." Today, we could say the same for most classrooms, "The children are supposed to all face the teacher." Of course the desks are not bolted down as they used to be and the furniture is moved about to accommodate different kinds of activities. But rarely are classrooms built and furnished to function as studios or workshops where children are to actively construct something.

Because long-held visions of classroom space dominate our thinking, I have found it useful to ask teachers to close their eyes and imagine a construction site. When we do this we see piles of debris, stacks of materials, an array of tools and equipment, a power source, and different-sized work surfaces. Every craftsman and artist studio has a variety of surfaces to work at, accessible places for storing a variety of supplies and materials, special equipment for holding, cutting, painting, connecting, and making, as well as sinks and bins for cleaning up. The construction site and studio are good metaphors for school space when students are actively engaged in applied literacy activities. When students use a multitude of primary and secondary sources, draft and edit documents, share ideas, and produce reports and displays, the school and classroom become

> part museum, publishing house, think tank, writers' workshop, artists' studio, theater, drafting room, computer lab, library, bookstore, gallery, recording studio, and more (Hartman, 2000, p. 282).

This kind of the classroom design was addressed in the mid-1990s by the Apple Classrooms of Tomorrow Project (ACOT). One aspect of the project focused on the physical environment needed to support "more interactive, collaborative, and inquisitive student-centered approaches to learning (Stuebing, Celsi, Cousineau, 1994). The ACOT project participants, both elementary and high school teachers, experienced real problems when they implemented technology-oriented student-centered learning in spaces designed for teacher-centered learning. These problems, as well as how they solved them, led them to develop a list of space requirements for future schools. Here are some of their suggestions for designing schools and classrooms that support student-centered inquiry-driven learning.

1. More diverse and flexible instructional space. Mini theatre-like areas where classes can meet together for presentations. Smaller studio-like production areas where teams can do word processing, access Internet, print, compose, edit, and prepare documents.

2. Acoustically sensitive space. Reduce sound interference with special acoustical treatment and special rooms for louder meetings and special rooms for quiet work.

3. More diverse furniture. Tables for group work, for production of documents and displays, accessible and secure storage cabinets for equipment, projects, and personal property.

4. Increase visual access with more office-like carrels and work stations. Employ flexible walls and more doors and windows to promote movement and communication.

5. Flexible placement of technology. Place electrical power sources to allow technology to be moved into the center of the room or placed on periphery.

6. More attention to physical comfort. Heating and cooling that meets all-year climate conditions. Aesthetically pleasing colors and adequate window coverings and lighting that controls glare and promotes presentation with technology-driven graphics.

In the ACOT project the teachers stressed that flexibility does not mean that all furniture and equipment is portable and that getting students to use educational technology is not the goal. Flexibility means that occasionally the equipment and space will be rearranged to accommodate long- and short-term activities that range from planned to spontaneous. The ACOT teachers said that computers, printers, digital cameras and projectors, and the Internet are only the tools they use to support learning. So they placed heavy and large technology and furniture in permanent and semi-permanent locations and used portable storage furniture and movable tables for smaller items like laptop computers, books, paper, and other supplies. Figure 5.1 shows a diagram of how a dream middle-grade classroom might look when the furniture and space are arranged to support applied literacy activities.

I realize this dream space may not be possible in many schools, but teachers are moving toward making their classrooms and schools more like workshops and studios. When they conduct applied literacy activities they find ways to add table surfaces for small group work, storage areas for materials, display areas in

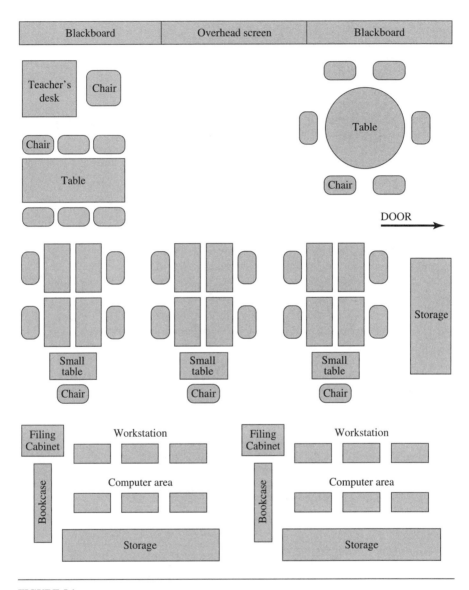

FIGURE 5.1

hallways, technology-based work stations, and places to present projects to live audiences.

In addition to new time and space considerations, the following section describes the roles of media specialists, parents, and individuals in the community in making reading and language arts authentic.

Role of the School Library Media Specialist

Successful applied literacy activities like those described in this book often feature a collaborative effort between teachers and the school librarian media specialist. Working together the teacher and the media specialist help bring to fruition the goals of *Information Power*, a 1988 position statement of the American Association of School Librarians and the Association for Educational Communications and Technology. The intent of *Information Power* (McCarthy, 1997) is to describe how to get all students to achieve full information literacy as effective users of ideas and information. Under the best of circumstances your school media center will be well stocked with resources including up-to-date information technology services via the Internet. Ideally your library has full-time school media specialists plus some assistants who work together with teachers to plan applied literacy inquiry activities in a setting rich with information resources. Ideally, your library features flexible scheduling so that users have open access to librarian media specialists and the library's resources.

However, while high school and middle school libraries may have full-time library media specialists, many elementary school libraries are not fully stocked, staffed, or technology-enriched. Far too many schools reflect a "big gym—no library" culture with neither a school library nor a media specialist. And, if an elementary school has a media specialist, he or she is not flexibly scheduled and has no support staff. The librarian and teachers function separately and students attend "library classes" that are viewed as enrichment or literature appreciation but not real learning. Part of this is due to the mindset that real learning only occurs in the classroom and the library is an "extra" feature of school. It is unfortunate that only some schools are able to fully address the lofty goals of *Information Power* in which McCarthy (1997) reported that less than half of the library media specialists in forty-eight library programs in New England believe that fully integrated media programs will enable students to achieve full information literacy for the twenty-first century. Reasons for this include the classic lack of budget support for personnel, materials, and space as well as the common practice of a part-time school librarian who follows a fixed library schedule. When classes are assigned to attend the library for up to five or six periods per day, the classroom teachers have "preparation" or "free" time. The fixed schedule plan means the library media specialist does not have time to collaborate with teachers and the library media resources are only available to the class that is in the library. Instead of using the library as a special classroom with a fixed weekly schedule, *Information Power* proposes that libraries be open and specialists be available to all students most of the time.

The shift to student-centered inquiry and the success of applied literacy activities rests on the availability of rich sources of information envisioned by *Information Power*. To see where your school is in regard to the vision for full information literacy use the following lists of role behaviors from the *Information Power* statement as a checklist. The checklist proposes that library media specialists have three interconnected roles: information specialist, teacher, and instructional consultant (DeGroff, 1996).

Information Specialist

In this role the librarian operates the library, follows a schedule, maintains the collection, and helps users take advantage of all the available resources. The information specialist:

- supports flexible scheduling during and after the school day for small groups and individuals;
- seeks input from students, and colleagues when selecting resources;
- assists students and colleagues in selecting, and locating books and information;
- assists students in developing systematic modes of inquiry;
- knows students' needs, skills, and abilities as well as teaching and learning strategies;
- knows about books and materials, and has accurate ways to locate information;

Library–Media Teacher

In this role the librarian teaches students and adults how to be information-literate. The library–media teacher:

- teaches students, colleagues, parents, and other adults how to locate books, resources, and information;
- promotes lifelong reading and learning, critical reading, and an appreciation for freedom of information;
- teaches a respect for and understanding of copyright and privacy laws;
- teaches parents and others techniques for reading with and to children.

Instructional Consultant

This role allows the librarian to work in concert with teachers to assure that library and research skills are integrated into the content areas. This role is the key factor in whether or not applied literacy activities are successfully integrated across the curriculum in the school. The instructional consultant:

- works with teachers to design applied literacy and content area instructional strategies;
- participates with teachers and students in selecting thematic inquiry projects;
- helps develop unit plans, gathers books and resources, and helps teachers and students carry out inquiry projects;
- helps assess student reading and inquiry habits and attitudes;
- plans, promotes, and helps assess the use of volunteer reading help for individuals and small groups of students.

Schools where Information Power is realized and teachers and students are able to successfully conduct inquiry projects shared several important features. The following list ranks them in order of importance (McCarthy, 1997):

- a strong library–media specialist committed to reaching out to teachers and providing a high quality program;
- support from administration and teachers;
- collaboration with teachers, and the use of the library media center them;
- an administration that provides budget and resource support;
- an educational philosophy or climate that encourages students to use information resources widely and to appreciate literature.

While the people, the technologies, and the sources of information in the school library media center are critical elements of school-based applied literacy activities, parents and people in the community also play an important role. The next section discusses the special role parents play.

Parent Roles

In addition to cooperation between teachers and library media staff, teachers report that support from parents is important to the success of applied literacy activities. How do they do this? They *inform* and seek parent *approval* of applied literacy topics, they ask parents to *share* their expertise, and they involve parents in *evaluating* applied literacy products and projects.

Inform Parents and Seek Their Approval

At the beginning of an inquiry project, when students are deciding which topics they will study, teachers send home a letter to the parents that explains the project, tells them what topic their child has selected, and asks them to express any concerns they may have about the project and the topic. Here is a sample letter:

Dear Parents,

This week Mr. Erickson and Mrs. Kelley are starting an inquiry project in social studies that features unsung local heroes. Students will be studying how different adults maintain and improve the quality of life in the local community through their leadership, their work, their volunteering, their hobbies, or other efforts. Students will be interviewing local people and preparing reports that describe how our community is helped by their efforts. We would like you to discuss this project with your child. When you have agreed with your child on whom he or she will interview, please sign the form and have your child return it to us by September 30.

(continued)

We are providing learning time at school for this project, but students are expected to work at home on this project for the next four to five weeks. The reading, writing, speaking, and listening activities they participate in and the report they produce is a major part of their grade in social studies and language arts for this grading period. Each student will have a tracking sheet that monitors his or her progress, and teachers will initial steps as they are completed. Later, we will send home a planning calendar so you can see how the project will progress. We hope this will help students complete their inquiry project and prevent problems such as falling behind or getting off track.

If you have any questions, please call either of us at school (222/532-1123). Thank you for your support in signing this and having it returned promptly.

Sincerely,

Mrs. Kelley and Mr. Erickson

My child, _____, would like to do research about

_____by

interviewing _____

Parent Signature_____

Parents as Resources

Very often parents are a rich source of information that teachers and students can tap when they are seeking information on a topic. For example, adults often possess special knowledge, skills, and experiences associated with work, hobbies, family culture, and travel. To tap this source teachers send letters to parents and others inviting them to describe how they might act as a resource. Here is a sample letter:

Dear _____

In order to provide students with a rich variety of primary sources of information, we are trying to identify people who have special knowledge, skills, and experiences. This is not an obligation. It is an opportunity for you to participate as a primary source for curious students. Here are some possible ways you can help:

1. Knowing about and valuing different cultures. Can you share your special nationality or ethnic knowledge through storytelling, music, special books, or a particular oral and written language? Yes _____. My special cultural interest is _____.

2. Work-related knowledge, skills, and experiences. Can you share particular information about your work-related activities that would be interesting to students? Yes _____. My work-related information is about _____.

8. Hobbies, Special Interests, Crafts. Can you share your special knowledge about your particular interest with students? Yes _____. I would be able to talk, demonstrate, or show students about _____.

Parents As Audience Evaluators

When students complete their applied literacy projects and present reports, debate, or perform, teachers invite parents and other interested adults to listen, observe, and critique the outcomes and products. Presenting and performing benefits both the students and the community. Instead of simply taking a test that is graded by teachers, the students are applying their literacy and inquiry skills and sharing their new knowledge in a real-life context with a much wider audience. By going "public," students feel that what they learned has practical value that goes beyond the privacy of a mark in a grade book. When parents and adults in the community, such as employers, see students applying their inquiry skills and sharing knowledge from both primary and secondary sources, they are assured that schools are preparing children for future schooling as well as life as future citizens.

School and Workplace Connections

In addition to gaining parent support, applied literacy projects that feature real-world texts can bridge gaps between schools and workplaces. For example, when applied literacy activities use real-world reading and writing materials, students get a glimpse of how literacy tasks look in the meaningful context of the adult work world. In addition, we know that the ability to comprehend school literature does not always transfer to understanding and using out-of-school repair manuals, tax forms, and assembly instructions. When students use out-of-school sources with help from teachers, they can gain literacy skills that do have great potential to become lifelong applications in the world of work. Here is a partial list of some real-world materials that teachers use with specific content areas (Mikulecky, 1989):

Science	Labels, Medicine Instructions, Weather Data, Lab Procedures
Social Studies	Contracts, Tax Forms, Atlas, Travel Pamphlets, Charts and Graphs
Mathematics	Receipts, Recipes, Financial Forms, Mileage Maps, Bank Statements
Industrial Arts	Manuals, Drawings, Estimates, Contracts, Trade Journals

A school in Michigan provides an example of an applied literacy activity that connected school and work. In grade six, students started building an employability portfolio (Stemmer, Brown, Smith, 1992). They prepared portfolios that documented their academic strengths, personal management performance, and teamwork abilities. The idea was not to see who was employable for a specific job, but provided them with a way to learn how to document personal growth and change in a world where changing jobs and careers is inevitable. Here is a sample of how their skills were profiled:

Academic Skills
- Read and understand text material, charts, graphs, and forms
- Understand basic math and demonstrate ability to apply math to problems
- Use research and library media skills
- Use tools and equipment
- Speak and write to conduct business
- Use critical thinking and scientific reasoning to solve problems

Personal Management Skills
- Attend school/work regularly and meet school/work deadlines
- Propose career plans
- Demonstrate personal self-control, and ability to attend to details, and stay on-task
- Ability to follow directions, work without supervision, and learn new skills
- Show initiative and suggest better ways to get jobs done

Teamwork Skills
- Actively participate by listening, expressing ideas, and volunteering to help
- Know and value group rules and norms
- Act as a leader or follower to achieve group goals
- Know when to compromise in order to achieve group goals
- Willingly work in changing settings with people of diverse backgrounds

Sixth grade is not too early to think seriously about future work. Although it is too early to make lifelong work decisions, it makes good sense to help children in early adolescence connect their current literacy activities to future work-related literacy skills.

Summary

Applied literacy activities demand less attention to school-oriented linear time concepts and more attention to circular and flexible time arrangements. Long-held classroom space concepts also change when students become active users of information. In this chapter examples of changes in time and space illustrated what happens when student-centered inquiry activities are implemented. Applied literacy activities also affect the roles of the school library media specialist, create new opportunities for parents to participate, and foster new school and workplace connections.

References

DeGroff, L. (1996, Spring). *Getting to know the school library media specialist.* Instructional Resource No. 25. Athens, GA: University of Georgia, National Reading Research Center.

Hartman, D. (2000). What will be the influences of media on literacy in the next millennium? *Reading Research Quarterly, 35*(2), 281–282.

Hlebowitsh, P. S. (2001). *Foundations of American education.* Belmont, CA: Wadsworth.

McAndrew, D. A. (1993). Richie, Alicia, and the new time of literacy workshops, *Journal of Reading, 37*(3), 164–168.

McCarthy, C. A. (1997). A reality check: The challenges of implementing information power in school library media programs. *School Media Quarterly, 25*(4), 205–210.

Mikulecky, L. (1989). Real-world literacy demands: How they've changed and what teachers can do. In D. Lapp, J. Flood, & N. Farnan (Eds.), *Content area reading and learning: Instructional strategies.* (pp. 123–136). Englewood Cliffs, NJ: Prentice-Hall.

Stemmer, P., Brown, B., & Smith, C. (1992, March). The employability skills portfolio. *Educational Leadership, 49*(7), 32–35.

Steubing, S., Celsi, J., & Cousineau, L. (1994). Environments that support new modes of learning. Online. Available at: acot@applelink.apple.com

Tyack, D. B., & Cuban, L. (1985). *Tinkering toward utopia.* Palo Alto, CA: Stanford University Press.

6

Multiple Information Sources

The teacher required each student to select a U.S. state to research. One student searched through her computer encyclopedia and produced not only her own report but also reports for her friends. The teacher was angry and considered it cheating. The mother said, "No, the assignment was too simple."

Caine & Caine, 1997

Middle-grade students and teachers are engaged in learning new ways to deal with life in the information age. The explosion of information is challenging all of us in education to question and rethink our assumptions about information sources, tools, and uses. When I began researching how students use information, it soon became apparent that in more and more classrooms the use of a single textbook with all the information "bundled" together for efficiency is changing. For the last fifty years the norm for literacy instruction is the "bundling of teacher edition, student edition, big flip charts, traded books, cassette tapes, flash cards, tests, and so on (Hartman, 2000, p. 281). In place of classroom activities, in which students comprehend and compose from a single text, teachers are designing situations in which students read, relate, and respond to multiple sources. When this occurs, students are often challenged and surprised by unexpected discoveries or conflicting information. Multiple sources cause students to revise old understandings and responses to previous texts in light of information from new sources. This decentralization of information has led me to rethink my own assumptions about the relationship between teaching and information, especially in regard to the notion that information is a commodity.

Information as Commodity

A basic fact of life for me as a teacher is that I have been trained, hired, and evaluated to transmit information. As I say this I am fully aware that teaching involves much more than the direct transmission of information. After thirty-some years I can still recall the father who told me that he wasn't interested in the books and the curriculum I had just described at the parent open house. He was mostly interested in what kind of a person I was as a teacher and how I was going to treat his fifth grader. The message he delivered to me that night over coffee and cookies in the cafeteria was, "Be a decent human being when you use those books with my child." And, while I've tried to do this, the bottom line is that I have spent my entire teaching life working in settings designed to deliver a commodity called "information" to students.

In this book the vignettes illustrate that, while the primary school commodity for teachers is information, students are exercising more control over topics, questions, sources, and applications. The move to empower students to apply and use literacy requires that students have more control over information sources and uses. This movement signals a paradigm shift. Historically, schools function as information factories producing students who read, learn, use, and store information that experts deem important. It's fair to say that we arrange, staff, and supervise classroom factories where we dispense age-marked or content-labeled packets of information for a fixed number of months. Likewise, libraries have functioned like central warehouses, storing information until teachers and students ask to use it. I don't think I'm going too far when I say that schools and libraries have traditionally been organized and staffed to facilitate the basic assumption that knowledge, in the form of packaged and school-board approved information, is a commodity generated by experts and dispensed by teachers and librarians.

When I talk like this to teachers in workshops or in my university classroom, they tell me this is a narrow and harsh view of school. But I find the picture of "school as factory and information as commodity" to be both accurate and useful in light of the widespread and rapid changes we are experiencing regarding information sources, uses, and controls. The truth is that the school and library do not have the monopoly on information they once had. My opening quotation is a metaphor for teaching and learning in the information age. I feel for the teacher who, shocked by her young students' access to knowledge, said they cheated. Whether or not you agree that the students cheated, I believe the teacher genuinely felt "cheated" because information—the commodity she usually controlled—was now free and available to anyone with digital access capability. Her old practice of telling students to fill up on information on a state or whatever is too simple, too primitive in the information age. The reason it is too primitive is simply that gathering information about a state, such as Alaska, is not knowledge because to "know" means the information, like puzzle pieces, only makes sense when it is related to a larger context. In order to qualify as knowledge, information about Alaska must relate to other information and satisfy some human social or psychological purpose or need. Instead of simply gathering information and writing a report on Alaska, students need to actively construct knowledge about Alaska that satisfies questions and concerns like:

Why am I doing this? Will this information be useful or interesting? Do I care about anything in Alaska? How is Alaska unique or similar to other places? And when students have a variety of questions and needs in mind, they need to access multiple sources because bundled references and single texts may not provide what they want to know.

Expanded Range of Sources

This chapter describes an expanded range of information sources beyond the approved textbooks that students and teachers typically use. Figure 6.1 provides a visual representation of what I mean by an expanded range of information for an individual.

The students in the center are close to typical school information sources that are developed by experts and approved by school officials. Approved school materials affect virtually all school lessons and clearly establish a climate in which information is a centralized commodity that teachers dispense to children. Around these centralized sources are a vast number of decentralized information sources that are openly available to everyone in the home and community. One fact that emerges from Figure 6.1 is that there are many more sources and kinds of information outside of school than in school. Another is that the figure is oversimpli-

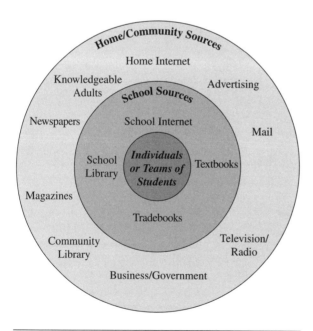

FIGURE 6.1

fied and omits many common sources like globes, maps, brochures, phone books, almanacs, reference books, manuals, dictionaries, thesauruses, charts, graphs, and so on. I could keep the list going but you already can see that the real problem here is that there are more information sources than we can possibly pay attention to.

One way to think about this is using a *push* and *pull* analogy. One half of the problem for teachers is how they can get students to pay attention to and learn the curriculum-based information the community is paying them to *push* at students. The other half is what teachers can do to help students *pull*, or inquire about, the life-based information that they desire. In a sense the *push* and *pull* analogy is what this book is all about, especially the *pull*, or inquiry side of learning. Later in this chapter I will describe a variety of information-rich sources that teachers help students use. But first, I'd like you to think about when we are and when we are not engaged by different sources of information.

Information Engagement

Most of the time we receive information passively. One reason we tend to stay dry even though a waterfall of information pours down around us is a survival response by our brain. If we were engaged and committed to all the information coming at us the result would be insanity. Another reason we tend to stay dry is that information is most often transmitted in a mode that does not always require us to respond. Even though we may pay attention while we view, listen, or read, there is often no emotional engagement or commitment to the information, so we remain passive and unchanged. Information theorists suggest that a hierarchy of information engagement exists that resembles a ladder (Davenport, 1997). At the bottom rung, the lowest engagement involves passively viewing, listening, and reading information as a single individual. A school example of this is a workbook activity. The next highest engagement rung involves talking about and discussing information with someone else. Higher on the ladder is arguing about and defending information, which is just below the next rung, presenting and teaching the information. The top of the engagement ladder involves simulation, games, or actions that require a direct, live activity in response to the information.

I was talking about this with a young teacher who tries to avoid using workbooks in her classroom because she strives to get children to respond actively, not passively, and said:

> In the movie *Apollo Thirteen* the astronauts had to respond quickly and correctly and use new information to repair their damaged moon mission vehicle—or they'd never get back to earth. That movie is the best argument against workbooks I can think of.

The point of all of this is that, in addition to helping students inquire and "pull" information more effectively, applied literacy activities can also help them learn critical literacy skills so that they are better equipped to handle information that is being pushed at them. If this is going to happen in schools, it will require examining both old and new information sources as well as primary and secondary information sources.

In educational circles, primary sources are publications in which researchers report results of their studies directly to readers. The most common ones I encounter in my work are journals like *The Journal of Educational Research*. Secondary sources refer to publications in which authors describe the work of other researchers. The most common secondary sources in schools are textbooks. For students in the middle grades primary sources of information may include voice recordings and direct quotes from people or live action and video recordings of events. In this book, primary sources include the lessons plans, teaching materials, and student products I have collected directly from schools. News reporters use original quotes to authenticate what they report. Television uses videotape to record actual events so they can authenticate what they report. On the other hand, secondary sources of information are usually a collection of primary information. In this book, when I refer to studies done by others I am creating a secondary source from someone else's primary information. Typically, schools use secondary sources. That is, someone collected and organized a set of primary source information and bundled it for school consumption.

One way to think about this is to use a meal metaphor. If you bake two pizzas from scratch, and serve them to your friends, the pizzas are primary sources of flavor and nourishment that you prepared. If you order take-out pizzas, pick them up, and serve them to your friends, they are secondary sources of food prepared by someone else. In school, when students interview knowledgeable people, for example, prize-winning chefs about how they prepare a special food, they are using a primary source. When they read books already written about famous chefs they are using secondary sources.

Typically, most school information sources are secondary. School texts, like the pizzas you ordered, come ready to serve and deliver content to students. If the information in a school text is interesting, unexpected, or exactly what the student is looking for it can be engaging. But secondary school sources can be bland and shallow, and the content is often decontextualized. So, even though school texts are designed to connect subject matter with children of particular ages and grades, they may or may not. Teachers are keenly aware of this and seek engaging secondary sources. A lot of teaching involves trying to motivate children and connect them to secondary information sources. On the other hand, students often connect quickly and easily with primary sources. The connection is quick when the information is related to their question or concern. The connection is easy because the information is fresh, direct, interesting, and sometimes unexpected.

However, primary sources and out-of-school secondary sources, like the uncooked flour, tomato paste, cheese, and other basic ingredients of a pizza, are not prepackaged for school consumption. So students need teachers who can help them locate, evaluate, organize, and prepare the raw information for public consumption. This requires special teaching and learning arrangements. Tapping a wider range of information sources, especially primary sources, requires new thinking and more effort by both teachers and students.

Primary Human Sources

Interviews

For her environmental science project eighth grader, Hannah, interviewed Joe Cohen, an Anna, Illinois, swimming pool contractor. She was involved in a science unit about how scientific information is applied to commercial products and businesses. In order to find information about how his construction business used scientific ways to keep swimming pool water clean, safe, and clear, she talked to Joe. He told me Hannah was shy at first but, after he helped her focus her questions, they were able to discuss topics like chemicals, filters, pumps, maintenance, laws, and other factors he knew about. The information she gathered was used to write and illustrate her science project on how science knowledge was used by a businessman like Joe. Her award-winning science fair display included photos and accompanying text of a pool filter, pump, and chemicals. Hannah's research project was a test that compared the effectiveness of chlorine and bacquacil on controlling algae. She took green, algae-contaminated water and treated it with the two chemicals and found that in one week the chlorine made the water clearer than the bacquacil. She measured changes in water clarity over one week with a Vernier colorimeter that was connected to a Macintosh computer. Data Logger software produced graphs that charted daily water clarity of the two treated samples for one week. Although her results favored chlorine she also noted that, based on all of her sources, as well as her own experience with her family swimming pool, a longer trial such as a month might have made led to different results. She noted that, because bacquacil is more stable and does not dissipate as fast as chlorine, a longer trial might have shown that the two chemicals were equally effective.

When I talked with Hannah about her project, I asked her how the interview went and she said that Mr. Cohen was very nice. She said he talked fast and, when she had trouble taking notes, he took the paper and pencil and wrote down his responses as he talked and answered her questions. When I talked to Mr. Blair, Hannah's teacher, about students' interviewing skills, he said he hadn't spent much time teaching students about interviewing because that had not been a problem. Fortunately for Hannah, her primary source was very accommodating and he took over the note taking. This may not always happen, so teachers have learned to prepare students for primary source interviews by spending time in class practicing questioning and note taking.

Teachers devote several days of classroom time showing students how to interact with primary sources. The teacher models an interview by interviewing another teacher and then the students practice reciprocal interviewing by taking turns asking each other about personal hobbies or favorite activities. They start with the basic questions of what, when, why, and how and move to follow-up questions to obtain more in-depth and interesting information. Sometimes teachers tape-record a practice interview and the class listens and critiques the dialogue. Together the teacher and students develop a list of tips for interviewing:

- let the person talk
- don't ask yes or no questions
- keep the interview on the topic
- ask both personal questions (When did you start developing your own photos?) and general questions (Do you know anyone who does this for a living?)
- ask follow-up questions that probe deeper into the topic (Have you ever had any problems when adding items to your collection?)
- take some brief notes while interviewing and write more complete notes soon after the interview.

The students and teacher also talk about asking for permission to use a tape recorder and the teacher shows them a microphone available at a local electronic store that can be easily attached to a telephone receiver to record phone interviews. Protocols for good phone manners are discussed and students practice mock phone interviews in class to get a feel for how to be polite, positive, and productive on the phone.

Going directly to a live source who has firsthand information is a powerful information-gathering activity for students in the middle grades, but teachers have to be flexible and ready for student reluctance and lack of experience. Here are some ways teachers introduce students to the idea of conducting face-to-face and telephone interviews.

- Watch the pros. Video- or tape-record expert reporters who do interviews on television and radio. Show the videos and discuss the questions that were asked and how the interviewer followed up to probe for deeper insights.

- Use the pros. Have a news reporter come to class and share interviewing experiences with students.

- Use the media. Have students make video- or audiotapes of interviews as homework. They can bring them to class for sharing and discussing.

Field Observations

John had his middle-school special education students take Polaroid pictures of potentially dangerous stairways, entries, doorways, driveways, and intersections in and near the school. The students wrote captions for the photos and made lists of safety tips and rules that addressed specific danger spots. The photos, captions, and rules were posted around the school to inform everyone and, perhaps, prevent accidents. The students received many accolades from fellow students, other teachers, and many parents for their work to make school a safer place. Field observations with cameras and videos were a good way for John's students to gather primary data for this thematic project on safety. The visual images prompted his students to read more about a topic and write specific, detailed paragraphs to accompany pictures.

In addition to collecting specimens, taking written notes, making rough sketches, or even measuring dimensions at an observation site, more and more schools have the technology to make pictures with digital cameras and videos. This enables primary visual data to be downloaded to computers for further communication purposes.

Primary Digital Sources

While the Internet is used primarily as a secondary source of information, the interactive nature of E-mail can be considered a primary information source. Teachers are still realizing the power and value of primary digital sources and research on school practices is ongoing. Rekrut (1999) reported on some successful uses of the Internet as well as providing some practical guidelines and cautions. For example, in spite of the obvious benefits of having fast access to a great deal of information, productive digital access for teachers and students requires detailed planning, parental approval, longer blocks of time, and special attention to book-marking sources. Some of the guidelines Rekrut offers include:

- Have clear instructional goals and try to determine if the internet sources are accessible.
- Place Internet lessons within the context of the existing curriculum.
- Understand the literacy demands and provide help so that vocabulary and comprehension problems are lessened.
- Have specific objectives for each session and be prepared to allow students more time to meet objectives.
- Have a written component such as a progress report of E-mail sent and received. This promotes accountability and helps manage and motivate as students see some results of their efforts.
- Publicize student findings on a school Web page, in public posters, or at public meetings.

The increased availability of digital information challenges us with many questions of access, use, accuracy, and information control. All of the uses and effects of highly decentralized information sources are beyond the scope of this text so I am limiting this section by focusing on the limited menu of purposeful E-mail.

Purposeful E-Mail

Within the context of planned lessons that are part of an ongoing school curriculum, teachers are finding that E-mail can be an effective primary source. E-mail is an umbrella term that covers a range of digital formats, audiences, and genres. Students can seek primary information directly from individuals, businesses, organizations, schools, and community and government agencies. They can instantly communicate in writing with fellow students in the same school as well as with others from around the world.

Fortunately, teachers do not have to "reinvent the wheel" to connect students to primary sources because many school-related Web sites are already up and running. A quick look at almost any professional teaching journal will provide lists of Web sites that have been checked for usefulness and reliability. The following addresses have an information literacy thrust and are just a sample of those that teachers have created. You can E-mail the teachers who've created the sites and get firsthand knowledge directly from the site creators or be put in contact with others who have firsthand information.

- New Internet users will find http://www.siec.k12.in.us/~west/online/index.html to be an excellent source of tutorials and examples of how to use technology in the elementary classroom. Even though the site has a primary grade focus, a new user in the middle grades will find this site valuable. It was created by Tammy Payton at Loogootee Elementary West in Indiana. The tutorials for creating Web sites are especially well done.

- Hazel's Homepage: http://www.marshall-es.marshall.k12.tn.us/jobe/ This site includes a variety of interesting links including assistance for getting started on the Internet. I have book-marked this site myself and have to watch out that I don't spend all my time there. Hazel Jobe, the vice-principal at Marshall Elementary in Lewisberg, Tennessee, developed the site and she is an excellent primary source.

- A great theme resource is http://www.stemnet.nf.ca/CITE/themes.html This site was developed by Jim Cornish at Gander Academy in Newfoundland. This model site contains links to Internet sites that support thematic studies, so using it helps avoid random surfing. It also links students to "safe" sites that are appropriate for children. Teachers and students can E-mail Cornish, a fifth-grade teacher, and get firsthand information about nonfiction thematic sources.

There are also sites that present more information on unusual and engaging types of primary sources like old photographs, documents, diaries, letters, buildings, clothing, artifacts, paintings, cartoons, posters, cemeteries, and so on. The National Archives Web site has many fascinating original documents on display, including: exhibits of photos from every decade in the last one hundred years, original documents of the most precious artifacts of our national history, spy documents from World War I, and original transcripts of communication from John Glenn's February 20, 1962 spaceflight on Friendship 7. The Archives Web site, http://www.nara.gov/exhall/exhibits.html, displays the line-by-line talk between Glenn and ground control. In the following copy it is interesting to hear this account of the reentry when the outer part of the space capsule burned off as it entered the earth's atmosphere at 80,000 feet.

> **CC (ground control):** Ah, Seven. This is Cape. What's your general Condition? Are you feeling pretty well?
>
> **P (Glenn):** My condition is good, but that was a real fireball, boy. I had great chunks of that retropack breaking off all the way through.
>
> **CC:** Very good; it did break off, is that correct?
>
> **P:** Roger. Altimeter off the peg indicating 80 thousand.

I have included additional Web site sources in Appendices C and D.

Other Primary Sources

Students can gather primary information from a variety of sources using their writing, speaking, and listening literacy skills. Examples of these kinds of information-gathering activities include: letter writing, conducting surveys, taking field trips, and attending civic meetings, classes, conferences, and courtroom sessions.

Letter writing. "Snail mail" is a good way for students to use formatted writing to gather primary information. Teachers can provide model letters that students can alter to fit their specific source. Before a final copy is mailed, students write a rough draft that is edited for content and writing protocols.

Surveys. Asking samples of people to respond to questions and ratings is a common practice in our culture. Everyday there is a popular media report that shares the results of a survey or poll on a current topic. Surveys tap representative opinions, ideas, preferences, and practices and are used to get a glimpse of what others are thinking. Students in the middle grades who conduct surveys learn the ins and outs of gathering this kind of information. They not only gain some information, they also have a better feel for the process and issues associated with the use and misuse of surveys. In addition, surveys and polls are an excellent way to apply mathematics to the information-gathering process. Surveys can be done by phone or face-to-face at school, at home, or in the community with individuals and small groups.

Samantha, a sixth grader interested in learning about school uniforms, surveyed students in grades six, seven, and eight at her school by asking, *Do you favor wearing school uniforms? Yes, No, Undecided. Please give some reasons for your answer.* She graphed response percentages by total responses, by grade, and by gender. Her results showed that most students said "no" and there were few differences between boys' and girls' responses. However, "yes" responses diminished as grade levels increased, leading her to conclude that younger students tended to favor uniforms more than older students did.

Surveys require careful planning. Here are some guidelines for helping students conduct, interpret, and share survey data.

- *Mass Media.* Collect your own or have students bring surveys they find in the mass media to class. Discuss how to interpret the data.

- *Respondents.* Teach students that sampling from a population requires asking oneself, "Who are the best people to respond to this specific survey question?"

- *Questions.* Provide practice for writing clear questions. Have students do mini pilot surveys to see if respondents understand the questions.

- *Data.* Provide practice in using mathematics data like percentages and averages, as well as some graphing and charting. Sports data is an excellent source for this. Simple Likert rating scales are also a way to add measurement ideas to surveys.

- *Objectivity.* Provide examples of objective questions that call for quantitative responses or definite choices. Compare objective with subjective questions that require explanations, opinions, and nonquantitative examples. Discuss the trade-off between objective question results that are easier to tabulate and subjective question results that often provide deeper insights into what people are thinking.

Field Trips.   Getting out of the classroom can be more than just a fun excursion, a vacation-like getaway. The authenticity of workplaces, adults at work or play, as well as natural settings, animals, and travel experience is engaging and contributes to authentic learning that lasts. Students are better observers when they are prepared beforehand to gather information on field trips. Before students get on the bus, they should be prompted about what to look for and what questions might come up. They should have sharp pencils, paper, and clipboards to take notes, as well as cameras to record scenes and tape recorders for interviews. Students often team up so one can ask questions, one can take notes, and another can take pictures.

One sixth-grade teacher planned ahead and had the students use stopwatches and the interstate mile markers to calculate speed in different combinations like miles per hour and miles per minute, feet per minute and feet per second, and so on. They used the feet per second measurement to discuss dangers like tailgating, and related rate of speed to choosing different routes and travel times. A fifth-grade teacher used a field trip to teach map-reading skills including directionality, location, distances, and map symbols. She prepared skeleton maps and students watched for landmarks, took notes, and added details to create more complete maps of the trip.

Going into the world invigorates our senses and wakes up our brains. We remember what we have done, what we saw, and with whom we talked. Creative teachers keep their eyes open for real opportunities to show students how to apply reading, writing, speaking, listening, and thinking outside the classroom.

Meetings, Conferences, Classes, and Courtrooms.   Another primary source of information for students is public meetings. Each week and month there are on-going city council meetings, zoning board hearings, local conferences on environmental issues, classes at local colleges, and, of course, legal activities in courtrooms. Careful planning beforehand, including parental permission, can insure that students will not be barred from attending or being admitted to sensitive or inappropriate settings.

These primary sources are only some places where students can go to gather firsthand information. In my research I have found teachers to be flexible and creative, as well as excited by their students' primary source activities. All of them offered the following advice: plan ahead, keep it simple at first, prepare students to actively gather information, expect mistakes, expect to reteach research skills, expect surprises, and look for the payoff in terms of motivated students.

Secondary Sources: Information-Cluttered Classrooms

I have found that teachers who engage students often have messy classrooms that overflow with information sources with applications outside school. The partial list of the kinds of sources you'll find in an information-cluttered classroom that follows includes newspapers and magazines, which are usually considered home and community sources. I have included them with school sources because more and more middle-grade teachers use them regularly in their classrooms.

Newspapers and Magazines

Many local newspapers have education programs that provide multiple copies of daily papers for classrooms. Magazines like *Ranger Rick* or *Time* or *Sports Illustrated for Kids* also have special subscription rates for classroom use. Teachers often start each day with a news review, teaching students about the different sections in the newspaper, and showing how the school curriculum and various lessons relate to the world beyond the school. These sources are good models for nonfiction writing, and teachers often have students write their own newspaper and magazine stories about real events that occur at school and in the community. Teachers also arrange for reporters to talk to students or be interviewed by students as primary sources who can provide good firsthand information about their work, their skills, and their motives.

Phone Books and Local Information Packets

The phone book is loaded with lots of information besides phone numbers. Zip codes, time zones, maps of local communities, and calendars of annual events are just a few of the kinds of data that is useful for research. The phone book is a great example of the use of categories and topic headings. Did you know that the Yellow Pages usually have more topic headings for *automobile* than any other topic? What is the second largest number of topic headings and what might we infer from this? One teacher had her students act like anthropologists. The "only" evidence they had about the civilization they were researching was the Yellow Pages. Frequency counts of headings led one team of students to infer that automobiles inhabited the civilization and that attorneys took care of them! Of course, the telephone book is also a great tool for locating and interviewing knowledgeable people. My son is a reporter and he says that, in addition to face-to-face interviews, the telephone book and the telephone are his major information-gathering tools.

Chambers of Commerce and city and town offices often have free packets of materials that are excellent sources of information for research on government agencies, businesses, industries, community leaders, and important officials. This information often describes tourist attractions, entertainment, restaurants, and art and cultural activities that reflect the quality of life that a community supports.

Maps, Globes, Atlases, and Satellite Photos

I personally love this stuff and like to keep track of wilderness places where I've backpacked and places I've vacationed. I have a detailed log and map of an eight-day float through the Grand Canyon on the Colorado River that I review so that I can relive the sights and sounds of that life-changing trip; the map engages me all over again. Students love to read, study, and mark maps of places they know.

There is a great children's book called *My Map Book* by Sara Fanelli (1995) that features Sarah's maps of her bedroom, school, and neighborhood as well as personal "maps" of her face, dog, and heart. Students who see this are often motivated to use the book as a model and make their own maps of real places they know. I recall an eighth-grade student who was completing a study skill workbook page on reading maps. When I asked him why he was taking time to correct the map of downtown Washington, DC, he said, "I used to live near here and this map is a little off." I also visited with a fourth-grade teacher who had the students make a series of ever-expanding maps. First they made a map of their classroom, then the school, then the city, the state, the United States, and so on. One parent came to school and located their room with his GPSI (Global Positioning Satellite Instrument) and the students loved to tell visitors the exact latitude and longitude of their classroom. Maps, atlases, and satellite images are available at local government agencies, geography departments in universities, outdoor equipment stores, the travel section in bookstores, as well as from the catalogs of the National Geographic Society.

Catalogs, Almanacs, and Other Fact Sources

These sources are packed with a range of fascinating factual information. Children love to search for specific facts about people, places, events, history, products, and whatever. One activity that promotes inquiry is to have a daily or twice weekly ten-minute "Did You Know" sharing time when students have a chance to share some new and interesting item with their classmates. These sources are especially good for the "pull" side of inquiry that flourishes in a cluttered classroom that honors curiosity.

Nonfiction Trade Books

Today, more than ever before, there are many new excellent nonfiction sources for middle-grade students. Check out the nonfiction publishers' booths at reading conferences and you'll find a gold mine of appealing sources that are both engaging and informative. For example, publishers like Scholastic, Time-Life Education, and the Grolier Classroom Publishing group of Children's Press, Franklin Watts, and Orchard Books are producing an enticing range of books on everything from primates to pop culture, Da Vinci to Duke Ellington, and Williamsburg to Web Site Construction. Many new nonfiction books are packaged in thematically arranged sets and feature excellent photography and readable text. One of my favorite formats features acetate overlays such as those in the book, *Castles,* by Baines (1995). The overlays enable readers to peer inside parts of the castle or view jousting knights from different angles.

When I see this new crop of nonfiction books I can't help but think that we are acknowledging that children's authentic interests are usually centered on nonfiction. When children begin to write they write nonfiction. Their early stories do not have plots, characters, and events or follow time sequences of beginning–middle–end. They tell about themselves, their life events, their families, and their pets because that is what they know. So it is good that a new wave of virtually unlimited kinds of nonfiction books are now available to help us connect literacy lessons and content studies with students' inherent desire to understand reality.

Reading researchers (Richgels, Tomlinson, & Tunnell, 1993) compared typical textbooks and nonfiction trade books and concluded that the trade books "contained longer, more complex sentences, achieved deeper elaboration of a smaller subset of topics, . . . than did textbook passages" (p. 161). They suggested that, because trade books had better text structure and coherence, they were more comprehensible than textbooks.

Case Study: Tim's Story

I've included in this chapter a case study I constructed that is intended to be used as a way to discuss some of the issues we face today as we move toward the use of multiple sources to engage students in authentic inquiry. In this case a middle-school social studies teacher attempted to engage his students in a discussion about life as a Civil War soldier by using authentic sources from his personal book collection. Some possible questions to ask when discussing this case study include:

- Could Tim have done anything to avoid criticism?
- Is Tim justified in using other secondary sources besides the school text?
- Do you see any openings for students to do research with primary sources?
- Is this case realistic?

Madison Middle School. Fifth Period. Tuesday, April 20.

Second-year social studies language arts teacher Tim Brand is walking to the teacher's lounge when Dr. Hadley, the principal, asks him to come into his office. Closing the door, Hadley says, "Tim, I got a call from a parent. Seems you read some gross passages to your third period class yesterday. One student was very upset by some gory details about the Civil War. She told her parents about it and they called to complain this morning. Can you tell me what you did that would have been so upsetting?" Immediately, Tim's mind flashed back to Monday's class when Misty complained. He guessed it was her father or mother who had called. Trying to decide where to start to tell his side of the story, he wondered if he should go all the way back to last Friday when Sharon asked him to look over the new social studies adoption over the weekend.

Room 224. Friday April 16. After school about 3:40 p.m.

Tim is looking ahead to the weekend when Sharon, the eighth-grade English and social studies team leader at Marcus Middle School walks in his room.

"Tim, here, take a look at the new history text and let me know on Monday what you think. Have a good weekend."

Sharon walks away; Tim clears his desktop by dumping the stack of tests into his green briefcase. The only school work he'd planned to do over the weekend was grade the tests but now Sharon wants him to review the new book.

"Doesn't she know I have a life outside of school," he murmurs to himself. Wishing that he had said it out loud to her, he reluctantly slips the book in with the tests, picks up the briefcase, and, as he turns out the lights, he wonders if he might find time late Sunday to skim the text. Thinking he may not, he starts to think of excuses he would have for Sharon on Monday.

In his second year teaching social studies at Marcus, Tim's situational excuse for not protesting Sharon's short notice review request is his untenured status. But he knows his personal, and most compelling, reason is his quiet demeanor. Tim rarely shows anger, tries to be the good listener, and is not always sure that his knack for getting along is always a good trait. He believes his easygoing ways are an asset for a middle-school teacher, but right now he wishes he'd told Sharon his review would be later than Monday.

Turning out the room lights makes him feel a little better; the past school week was a good one by his standards. By the time he gets to his car he is only thinking ahead to dinner with friends and Saturday's golf game with Andy and Jack.

Tim's apartment. Sunday evening. April 18.

At 8 P.M. Tim makes a bag of microwave popcorn, pours a Dr. Pepper over ice, and takes the new text out of his green canvas case. As he begins looking at the text he recalls how some students call social studies "social slops" and how they groan when he makes reading assignments. He wonders, will this book be more or less interesting, harder or easier to read, up-to-date, and will it fit the curriculum?

Not wanting to spend too much Sunday nighttime on the new book he decides to look at the Civil War section that matches the material he will soon be teaching. Instead of a lame excuse for Sharon, Tim settles for a "quick and dirty" review so he'll have something to say to Sharon the next day.

Tim turns to a section titled *"Life in Wartime"* in the Civil War section. As a Civil War buff he has visited several battlefields including Gettysburg, Antietam, and Shiloh. He notices that the page in the new book has three prereading questions and eight vocabulary words placed at the top of the page. The teacher's guide tells him to remind the students to look for answers to the questions as they read and have them look up the words in the glossary before reading. Another note tells him to remind the students that many soldiers were not much older than they are right now. It tells Tim to ask students, how would you feel about fighting in a war right now? How would your families feel?

Tim scans the text looking for answers to the prereading question, "What was life like for soldiers during the Civil War?" Tim sees that, like most social studies texts, the authors provide a minimum of information about the youth of the new recruits, instances of friendly talk between Rebs and Yanks, the likelihood of death and injury from musket balls and cannon shells, and the crude medical care. There are only two quotes from soldiers in one whole page of the student text. "When I teach this I must add some primary source material from my Civil War books." Tim likes his students to hear primary sources and immediately gets an idea.

Setting the popcorn bowl aside, he goes to his bookshelf and picks up the new book on Shiloh, *Shiloh: The Battle That Changed the Civil War* (L. F.

Daniel, 1997), to look for some soldiers' letters or other reports that describe what life was like at the deadly Shiloh battle. He reads, "On April 6–7, 1862, 65,000 Union and 44,000 Confederate troops met on the banks of the Tennessee River. Nearly 24,000 were killed, wounded, missing. After an initial successful surprise attack by the Confederates the Union forces counterattacked. It was the bloodiest battle of the war. At the time right after the battle it didn't seem like the Union had gained any territory. But later the terrible losses by the Confederates enabled the Union to control the railroad system at Corinth, Mississippi and later secure the western territories all the way to Vicksburg."

Tim skims. Using a highlighter, he marks several passages that he could read to his students to give them a more detailed look at what life was like at a Civil War battle.

> Sergeant R. A. Oliver of the 17th Louisiana wrote that 'the trip back to Corinth used me up worse than the battle as we were gone five days and slept about ten hours during the time. We ate nothing almost, traveled very hard, and it rained on us every night' (p. 295).
>
> Private R. L. Davis of the 47th Tennessee wrote: 'We have been out of anything to eat but two crackers per day since Sunday morning & traveled in water & mud waist deep all day' (p. 295).
>
> At the Michie farm a general hospital with nearly four hundred patients had been established. A New Orleans journalist witnessed the grotesque sight: 'Arms, legs, hands, and feet, just amputated lay scattered about.' There were only two days' rations for the men, and no forage for the animals (pp. 295–296).
>
> An Indianapolis correspondent wrote that at one gun battery every horse was stretched out on the ground. The stench was intolerable. Another correspondent counted two hundred Rebel dead in the space of one acre. In one field, the remains of a Confederate gun battery were found, with thirty bodies and thirty dead horses in an area fifty feet square (p. 298).
>
> A union surgeon, Robert Murray, arrived at the battleground to find 6,000 wounded, with no bedding, no food or cooking utensils, and no table furniture. It proved impossible to find tents, and many of the wounded lay exposed to the rain on Sunday and Monday nights (p. 298).
>
> On April 8, a Confederate officer requested permission to send men through the union lines to bury the Southern dead. Grant, the Union general wrote: 'Owing to the warmth of the weather I deemed it advisable to have all the dead of both parties buried immediately' (p. 299).
>
> Wilbur Crummer worked in a party to collect dead bodies. The Rebels were buried two deep in a trench sixty feet long and four feet deep. The only monument was a sign carved with Crummer's pocketknife: '125 rebels.' The sign over the union trench read: '35 Union' (p. 300).
>
> 'The Railroad platform is almost covered with coffins and wounded soldiers— every train brings some anxious parent looking after their sons,' wrote a soldier. A Louisianan passed a church filled with wounded. He saw a large box in the back of the church, 'filled with feet and arms & hands. It was so full that 2 horrible & bloody feet protruded out of the top' (p. 302).

After reading about the carnage and death Tim thinks a better question for a study of war is "What was death like for soldiers during the Civil War?" Deciding to stop working, Tim puts the Shiloh book and the new text from Sharon in his canvas bag. He is not sure what to tell her, except that he has never seen a single text that provided students enough details to get them engaged in reading, much less answer questions like, "What was life like for . . . anyone from the past?"

It was later, while washing the popcorn bowl and cleaning up before going to bed, that Tim decided to try out both the new text and the quotes from the Shiloh book on his students on Monday. They would soon be studying the Civil War. They had the old book. His idea was to have the students read the old text and a copy of a page from the new text. He would also read some of the quotes from the Shiloh book. He would ask the students what they thought about the old, the new, and the quotes. Then he would have something to say to Sharon about the new text.

Room 224. Monday April 19. Third Period.

Tim decides to try out the old and new book and the quotes on his third period class because they are not shy about almost anything. Thinking they will give him something to say to Sharon, he passes out copies of the page from the new text and has the students find the section in the old book. They skim and read, trying to answer the question on what life was like for Civil War soldiers. There is a subdued discussion and some students tell about battlefields they have visited but no one volunteers a direct response to the question about how they would feel about fighting in a war at a young age. Tim tells them about how the textbooks cannot go into detail and then reads the quotes out loud.

The class sits quietly at first, but soon there are murmurs of "gross," and Misty says, "I'm getting sick—boxes of feet, yuck." "Misty is trying to get out of class again," says Sam. "Reminds me of a program I saw on Bosnia," says Joan. "They found mass graves where hundreds of people were buried together. I saw piles of bodies all stuck together. It gives me nightmares. Why do we have to see death and read about it all the time anyway?"

Matt answers her with, "If we want to answer the question about what life was like during the Civil War, or any war, we have to know about the horrible stuff." "Yeah," says Barbara, "I agree. If we want to have peace we need to know how horrible war is." Steve chimes in with, "My grandfather was in Vietnam but he won't talk about it. Last year, I asked him what he did there and he told me he couldn't talk about it." Later, I told my mom and she said it makes him sad and angry so the family doesn't bug him about it."

Pleased by the discussion, Tim asks, "Did the sources help answer the question about what life was like for soldiers? Did anything—the old book, the new book, the quotes I read—help more than the others?" "Well," said Janeel, "just like the Bosnia TV stuff that Joan saw, the battle quotes about bodies, graves, and body parts that you read helped me see how horrible battles are." "You shouldn't have read that gross stuff to us, Mr. Brand," says Misty. "I don't need to hear that to know life can be horrible for soldiers fighting in wars." "Don't be such a baby about it," says Sam. "I saw a dead guy after a car wreck last month by my house and it didn't bother me."

Sensing that the class might get into trading personal stories, and seeing that time was just about up, Tim tried a new question. He wanted to get some idea of how effective the new text and the primary source material he had read compared with the old text. "Do we all agree that life was horrible at Shiloh for both the union and confederate troops?" There was no protest so he went on. "Notice how the different sources talk about different parts of a soldier's life in the Civil War. It wasn't all bad, was it? No, they weren't killing and being killed all the time. But don't we have to agree that when there were battles the soldiers' lives, or rather, deaths were horrible? Even if they were not killed they had horrible wounds and they suffered from amputations, starvation, and rain and mud. Could we say that battles made life horrible for Civil War soldiers?" "Yes," said Steve, "I think that's why my grandfather won't talk about Vietnam. I think the stuff you read from your Shiloh book is important to know. In a few years I could be old enough to be in the army and I hope I never have to be in a battle and see bloody body parts."

Monday, April 19. Fifth Period.

During his free preparation period Tim goes to see Sharon. He wants to report on the new text. He wants to tell her about the great discussion that took place. He wants to tell her about how the new text needs to be supplemented with original sources. Sharon is not in her room and, when he asks another teacher, she says, "Sharon is not here right now, she's at a meeting in the central office. Tomorrow she's going to a regional task force on testing but she'll be here Wednesday."

Tim thinks to himself, "Great, I spend Sunday night to be ready for Sharon and then she isn't even around. I should have waited." He walks to the teacher's lounge, gets a Dr. Pepper from the machine, and goes back to his empty room to get ready for the last two periods.

Room 224. Wednesday, April 21. Third Period.

Tim is in the back of his classroom picking up a stack of papers when Sharon enters and says, "Hey, I just talked to Dr. Hadley. Why did you upset your kids with those graphic war quotes? Hadley said it had something to do with my asking you to check out the new social studies book. I told him you were going to look at the new book, that's all. I told Hadley we were supposed to use the approved text, not other stuff that could upset kids and parents."

Tim is tempted to remain calm, but he can't stop remembering the discussion about the horror of war, the way the students saw why a Vietnam veteran didn't want to talk. He was convinced his quotes had been the key to the engaged discussion and the connections.

"Sharon, I'm convinced the approved text is a good start, but you know as well as I do that the text covers so much it cannot provide the intimate details that engage and hook the reader. Don't we want the students to think and care? As far as I'm concerned, I am going to keep supplementing the text with other sources, especially primary sources like those quotes. Those kids responded very maturely to the material. Sure, it was horrible stuff about body parts. But it isn't even as graphic as many movies today and the television news has stuff worse than that in color at 5 and 10 every week night. I had the best discussion about what life was like, no—DEATH IS LIKE—for soldiers in battle. These kids are not too young to deal with it."

"You have to stick with the approved material, Tim. Your job is not to upset the students with adult material you bring from home." Sharon turns and walks out, leaving Tim with the student papers in his sweaty hands.

Tim walks to his desk, puts the papers in his basket, and sits down. Looking out the window, he thinks it's ironic that he should get into trouble with the principal and his department chair over what he thought was excellent teaching. He muses about academic freedom and approved textbooks and wonders if he should have waited until he had tenure before he tried to motivate and engage students with primary sources.

Reflecting on Tim's Story

Should teachers play it safe and stick with approved sources? Some teachers who read this story say that rookie teachers should first "get credibility" before they take risks. Other teachers say that Tim should have sought approval before using his own book. Others say that they are not afraid to do what Tim did and are prepared to defend their actions. What anyone thinks about this depends on their disposition, the culture and climate of the school where they teach, and the values and tastes of the school and its community. Whatever you decide about Tim's story, the fact remains that the range of information sources available for students has dramatically expanded in the last decade. Teachers and librarians who seek to engage students with authentic sources need to consider the risks and proceed with their eyes wide open.

Summary

This chapter examined some of the assumptions about schools and teachers from an information-dispensing perspective and described the shift that teachers are making to teach middle-grade students how to use primary and secondary sources much like historians, reporters, and writers do. Examples of primary sources that are engaging for students include interviews, field observations, digital sources, surveys, field trips, meetings, conferences, and courtrooms. Examples of secondary sources include: newspapers, magazines, telephone books, maps, atlases, reference material, and the increasing number of attractive and engaging nonfiction trade books.

Expanding the range of information sources for students is not without its risks, and teachers and librarians have to consider their own credibility, their students' maturity, and the broader school and community disposition toward inquiry.

References

Baines, F. (1995). *Castles*. New York: Franklin Watts.

Daniel, L. F. (1997). *Shiloh: The battle that changed the Civil War*. New York: Simon & Schuster.

Davenport, T. H. (1997). *Information ecology*. New York: Oxford University Press.

Fanelli, S. (1995). *My map book*. HarperCollins.

Hartman, D. K. (2000). What will be the influences of media on literacy in the next millennium? *Reading Research Quarterly, 35*(2), 276–282.

Rekrut , M. D, (1999). Using the Internet in classroom instruction: A primer for teachers. *Journal of Adolescent & Adult Literacy, 42*(7), 546–557.

Richgels, D., Tomlinson, C., & Tunnell, M. (1993). Comparison of elementary students' history textbooks and trade books. *Journal of Educational Research, 86*(3), 161–171.

7

Guiding Students to Evaluate Information

It must be true, it was on TV, and then I found it on the Internet.

Jack, 6th Grade

This chapter features lessons and activities that focus on providing novice researchers with some critical thinking tools. Critical thinking involves "reasonable, reflective thinking that is focused on deciding what to believe and do" (Norris & Ennis, 1989, p. 1). The phrase "deciding what to believe and do" lies at the heart of the kind of critical thinking activities I selected for this chapter. If we are to help students think critically, we must provide a setting where students can defend choices about the information they believe or disbelieve. Making and defending these choices rests on the ability to "determine the relevance of information, distinguish between fact and fiction, perceive bias, form an opinion of the author's competence or the work's artistic merit, and detect logical flaws" (Perin, 1998, p. 69). In the following language arts lesson (Douglas & Dobos, 2000) notice how seventh graders discovered bias when they read conflicting accounts of the same event in history textbooks.

Vignette: Inform or Persuade

Seventh-grade teacher, Carol Dobos, and researcher Nancy Douglas (Douglas & Dobos, 2000) found two sixth-grade textbooks that presented noticeably different interpretations of American involvement in the Spanish-American War. One text (Patterson, Patterson, Hunnicutt, Grambs, & Smith, 1967) glorifies American involvement while another (Bass, 1991) discusses the role of the "Yellow Press" and concludes that America's involvement was a hasty decision. Because the students were seventh-grade above average readers, the different views of history were judged to be discernible enough in these sixth-grade texts, so students could discover them by themselves. Finding two different versions of a topic is the most difficult and time-consuming task for this kind of lesson. Dobos and Douglas suggest that one way to solve this problem is to select an older text and one more recently published, although two current texts could present different versions. The topic or issue is not as important as having two different versions of a topic that is new to the students. They also stressed that, while some newer texts sometimes overtly present conflicting points of view to intentionally show students how to compare excerpts, they wanted students to discover differences on their own. They made enough copies so that about half of the students read one version, and half read the other version.

Before the students read the excerpts, Dobos had the class discuss why people write, and they came up with three reasons: to inform, to entertain, and to persuade. They brainstormed examples for each category.

Inform	*Entertain*	*Persuade*
texts	fiction	ads
dictionaries	television	bumper stickers
nonfiction	cartoons	magazines
Web sites	movie scripts	editorials

Before students read, Dobos provided background information, vocabulary, and a purpose for reading: Did America do the right thing by becoming involved in the Spanish-American War? Students read, highlighted the selection, and wrote an answer to the question. Responses were discussed and, as expected, the students who read the positive version said America was justified. When Dobos asked why, only half the room agreed with this, and the students who did not agree began to respond. A heated discussion took place and the teacher suggested that maybe the two texts were different. Students eagerly asked to read the other selection so that they could see whether the two texts were different.

After the students had a chance to read both passages, Dobos directed the students to look back at the list of purposes for writing they had generated earlier and asked them if textbooks still fit under the inform category. Their response was overwhelming and they moved texts to the persuade category.

Dobos and Douglas were emphatic that all students did not draw the same conclusion nor did this lesson teach critical thinking. They said that this lesson only pointed out that texts might not be neutral sources of objective truth and that one needs to take the time and spend the effort to consider if the text is trying to inform, persuade, or entertain. They said that this type of learning activity helps students to see for themselves that history books contain interpretations of history along with the facts. This is an important first step in helping students develop a disposition to think critically when they read textbooks.

Teaching children to read critically is not an easy task when we consider that middle-grade students are not only novice learners, they are children who are expected to read, listen, and learn worthwhile information from teachers and texts. Students are not expected to decide whether or not this information is valid. Their task is to study the information, make sense of it, remember it, and, hopefully, use it. There is widespread agreement that much of the information dispensed at school is inherently worthwhile, so there is no need to have to decide whether or not to believe it. However, we do know that information comes from many sources, and, while we might be inclined to trust school information, we know there is a lot of information that is unreliable. The decision to help students acquire tools for thinking critically about information is worthwhile, but it is not an easy goal to reach. One reason offered for this is that middle-grade students have limited experiences with judging the reliability and validity of print and media information. While I tend to agree, the encounters with children and teachers in the middle-grades that I document in this book are convincing evidence that the middle grades are a good place to begin the journey toward full literacy maturity.

Can We Teach Critical Thinking?

I am convinced that, if we accept the challenge and attempt to teach children to evaluate print and media information, we should do so with our eyes wide open. There are several difficulties to consider.

Critical thinking is difficult to teach because it clashes with what most of school tries to do. Providing students with tools for deciding what to believe and do with information is almost counterproductive to providing students with strategies for learning, remembering, and using information from a single source. Once we open the critical thinking toolbox, where do we stop? What school information do we accept without question and what information do we reflect on and possibly reject? For teachers the problem is crucial. If our students critically questioned everything we said and asked them to do, would we ever have enough time?

Another reason critical thinking is hard to teach is that we humans generally strive for consistency among our beliefs, and our reasons for believing and acting usually have more to do with what we already believe than new evidence or good arguments. There is a consistent research base that indicates students do not learn new information when it conflicts with their preexisting beliefs. The bottom line is that we rarely give up old ideas when confronted with new evidence. If this is so, should we even try to provide our students with tools to overcome these tendencies? Is there any way we can help students sort good information from bad information? Consider the following vignette as a starting point for answering these questions.

Vignette: Believability

Mary Anne kicked off her study of critical reading by passing out copies of two E-mail messages. She told her eighth-grade social studies and language arts students to read each one, decide which message was most believable and which one was least believable, and give reasons for their decision. Here is what the paper looked like with the messages.

1. Last week, in St. Louis, Missouri, a couple reported to the police that they came out to the parking lot behind their apartment and another man in a car near their car asked them for a jump start because his car battery was weak. He said he was in a hurry to get to the airport to catch a flight so they helped him start the car. He was very grateful and he made them take two tickets to a Blues Hockey game that night as a reward for helping him. They went to the hockey game and when they came home after the game their apartment was ransacked and their computer, TV, stereo, appliances, jewelry and cash were gone.

2. Sources at the St. Louis police department report that during July and October, when there is a full moon, someone hides under cars in the Wal-mart parking lots on the city's west side and grabs women's ankles when they return to get into their car. So far there have been three attacks but all of the women were able to get into their car and drive away to prevent further harm.

The most believable message is _____ / The least believable message is

_____

Reasons for believing/disbelieving are:

Mary Anne waited for five minutes while the students completed the task. She had them exchange papers and then tallied the responses from each student. She found that seventeen students said the first message was the most believable, while seven said the second one was the most believable. The discussion about reasons was very lively. Some claimed they had heard about the first one on the news but they had not heard the second one. One student said the second one was real because they knew someone who knew the name of a victim. The students started telling other victim stories as evidence to bolster their choices. One student said the first one was more believable because the events "all fit together" for her while the "full moon" was a tip-off that it was "just another ghost story."

As the class time grew short, Mary Anne told them that both E-mail messages were examples of "urban legends" or untrue stories that get passed from person to person. She said that these stories are often localized to make them more believable, they have been around for a long time, and they will continue to travel from person to person. She ended the lesson saying, "Often they travel orally but now the Internet is full of stories that get believed and passed on." Mary Anne told her class that, because the Internet is full of both good and suspect information, the class was going to learn how to evaluate Web sites. They would be spending about two days per week learning some ways to recognize misinformation when they do research on the Internet.

Helping Students Cope with Information

All of us have to cope with an increasing flood of information from organizations, groups, and individuals trying to promote and persuade us to pay attention to an event, a product, a perspective, or a political agenda. When we read "You May Already Be A Winner" on the sweepstakes envelope, we can either believe it, open the envelope, follow the directions and wait for our prize, or we can choose not to believe it and dismiss the sweepstakes offer as just another piece of junk mail. So much information pours down on us from everywhere that it's a good thing we have a two-sided brain to help us cope.

How the Brain Believes and Disbelieves

Neuroscientist V. S. Ramachandran (Ramachandran & Blakeslee, 1998) has an interesting perspective on how the left and right hemisphere work together to help us cope with all of the detailed information that bombards the brain every instant we are awake. If we didn't have a way to sift through the information and make some sense of it by fitting it into our preexisting belief system, we would always be revising our worldview and the chaos would drive us mad. What Ramachandran suggests, in an admittedly oversimplified fashion, is that the left hemisphere works to preserve our existing schema by either ignoring new information that doesn't fit, or by distorting it and squeezing it to make it fit. Meanwhile, the right hemisphere's function "is to play 'Devil's Advocate,' to question the status quo and look for global inconsistencies" (Ramachandran & Blakeslee, 1998, p. 136). We deny the sweepstakes offer if our stable belief system says that the odds are so against us it is silly to play. On the other hand, if our stable belief system is that we have a chance, we fill out all the forms, return them, and wait for our prize. Either way, the left hemisphere is at work keeping us consistent, and everyday we effortlessly either deny or accept new information and act in a way to maintain our stability.

However, what if our stable belief system is challenged by new information that is difficult to deny or squeeze in to make it fit? When the new information reaches "a certain threshold, the right hemisphere decides it is time to force a complete revision of the entire model and start from scratch" (p. 136). For example, suppose we are predisposed against gambling, but new "inside" information is introduced that is very convincing. In this instance the right hemisphere can force a paradigm shift that leads us to alter our belief system and place our bet.

Another perspective on belief and disbelief is provided by ongoing psychological research (Bower, 1991; Gilbert, 1991). Writing about gullibility and skepticism, Bower reported that research supports the notion that humans find it easy to believe and difficult to doubt what they read and hear. When people are presented with true and false sentences they generally take less time to determine the accuracy of the true statements. Researchers studying this phenomenon have pointed out that when people read assertions their true-false index arrow is pointed at true. The evidence suggests that it takes more psychological energy to be skeptical than it does to be gullible. All this suggests it's no wonder the supermarket tabloids are believed, why millions respond to their sweepstakes letters, and why misinformation on the Internet is accepted and passed on.

What Can Teachers Do?

Recent research studied fifth graders' use of inquiry with nonfiction trade books to study U.S. history (Vansledright & Kelly, 1998). While the students preferred the trade books over their class textbook, they did not note differences in form and content between the two types of text nor did they attempt to read them differently. The students did not have concerns about the validity or historical significance of any of their sources either. A related finding was reported for tenth-grade students who used multiple sources to study history (Stahl et al., 1996). Students in that study relied mainly on the first source they read and tended to ignore conflicting information in later readings. The authors concluded that, unless high school students get specific instruction in how to integrate information from different texts, they may not benefit from studying multiple historical sources.

I think you'll agree with me that the tendency to accept, rather than doubt, the first information we read and hear is rather daunting information for teachers, especially when we know that some sources, like the Internet, are not peer-reviewed or subject to verification. Do we have the time, and what tools can we give novice researchers to help them overcome the natural tendency to believe the first source they read and hear?

Helping Students Evaluate Sources

Beginning in the middle grades, when student curiosity and interest in nonfiction begins to flourish, teachers are planning lessons that teach critical thinking skills. For example, biographies are excellent sources for helping students handle conflicting information. The reason for selecting biographies is that it is not uncommon to find that different accounts of famous people will have conflicting information that begs either to be resolved or at least acknowledged. In the following vignette, consider how the students and the teacher handled conflicting information about a famous person.

Vignette

Seventh graders Shawna and Grace, while researching biographies in a language arts–social studies unit on the Great Depression, find two different sources on the work of photographer, Dorothy Lange. She is famous for her photos depicting the hardships of the Depression, especially the one of a mother and her children facing famine after a pea crop failure in California. One source repeatedly says that, after taking photographs of people hit hard by the Depression, she "ran" to her editor with the pictures. Another source describes how Lange had polio as a child, had a severe limp, and had difficulty walking. With help from their teacher they write a new biography of Lange that combines both sources. The new biography omits the image of Lange running in a hurry to get her work published.

One could claim that the seventh graders have constructed a new biography that combines both sources and portrays Dorothy Lange more accurately than either of the original two sources.

When students find conflicting information they do what adults often do: they search for more evidence that may reconcile the conflict. For example, seventh-grader Diana wrote, "One thing I found while doing this research is that one article said General William T. Sherman was born on February 8, 1820 and the other said he was born on May 8, 1820. I checked his birthday in other sources and the February date seems right." In the two previous examples the running and the date discrepancies were discovered by the students, and the teacher had not foreseen them and had not planned to deal with the discrepancies ahead of time. Should teachers count on natural discrepancies to appear or should they orchestrate lessons in which conflicts exist? The obvious answer is that we should do both. We should be ready to help students deal with what they uncover on their own and we should plan lessons that contain conflicting facts, opinions, and explanations. Conflicting birth dates may prompt us to try to read more to find out what is correct but such discrepancies may not spur us to further investigation.

> The truth that matters the most to people is not factual truth but moral truth: not a narrative that tells what happened but a narrative that explains why it happened and who is responsible (Ignatieff, 1997, p. 17).

Facts like conflicting dates do not matter to us as much as why things happen or who is responsible. Therefore, if we want to engage students and give them tools for handling discrepancies, we must provide structured lessons in which we model how students can attempt to resolve interesting and potentially significant discrepancies. An example from a sixth-grade class will illustrate how a teacher helped students use inference to explain conflicting information about spiral staircases. Inferential thinking and group discussion are important tools we need to use when texts do not fully explain why something happened and who is responsible.

Spiral Staircase Mystery

The teacher passed out multiple copies of the nonfiction book, *Castles,* by Baines (1995). It is an attractively illustrated book that features detailed illustrations along with text that describes the functions of particular parts of castles. Page 12 shows a cutaway view of a corner tower of a castle that encloses a spiral staircase. The text next to the illustration reads:

> Spiral staircases usually rose clockwise. This meant that an attacking soldier who was climbing the stairs would find it difficult to use his sword.

The teacher also gave the class a copy of dialogue from a television travel show on Scottish castles.

> In my tour of Great Britain I noticed that in most castles the spiral staircases located inside the corner watchtowers turned to the right, rising in a clockwise fashion. However, in Scotland I was in two castles where the spiral staircases turned to the left, rising in a counter clockwise fashion.

She had both texts read aloud and wrote two questions on the chalkboard:

- Why did castle builders have the spiral staircases rise in a clockwise fashion?
- Why would the Scottish staircases rise in a counterclockwise direction?

She asked two students to act out a sword fight between an attacker and a defender and then launched a whole-class discussion with the following prompts:

- Imagine you are using a sword to either defend or attack a castle.
- Why would it be easier to defend a spiral staircase that curved upward in a clockwise fashion?
- Why would it be difficult to attack going up a spiral staircase that curved in a clockwise fashion?

There was a lively discussion about sword fighting, and the teacher had to ask students to keep some order, give everyone a chance, and listen to each other. After about five minutes, she had one student begin to record assertions and explanations on the chalkboard using the following array:

Spiral Staircases in Castles   *"Why?"*   *"Who?"*
Most curve upward clockwise to the right
Two in Scotland curve upward counterclockwise

The sword fighting simulation, the discussion, the recording of ideas, as well as teacher prompts about right- and left-handedness and inherited family traits, enabled the sixth-grade students to infer that most people are right-handed and, consequently, swinging a sword with the right arm gives a defender look-ing down a staircase that twists clockwise to the right the advantage. Right-handed attackers going up the staircase would find it difficult to use their right arms because the wall restricts their right side. On the other hand (no pun in-tended), the Scottish castles had staircases that curved the other way because left-handedness was an inherited trait in the families that lived there. They could defend their castles easier because swinging their swords from the left side was easier in staircases that curved the other way. One student quipped that maybe some invaders had special left-handed fighters who could fight their way up clockwise curved staircases. Another student concluded, "They were really smart way back then to build castle staircases this way."

Conflicting information is appealing and engaging to middle-grade stu-dents and provokes them to practice inferring and the critical thinking needed to evaluate the credibility of content. In the examples cited so far, conflicting in-formation from books, television, and typical print media have been featured. In the next section there are lessons for evaluating information from the media.

Media Literacy and Popular Culture

While most states have recently added a call for media literacy instruction to their curricular guidelines, classroom instruction in the United States has "lagged far behind other English-speaking countries" (Kubey & Baker, 1999). The real-ization that we spend as much as nine to twelve years of our lives in front of a television set is prompting schools to teach students how to interpret visual media. In addition, middle-grade teachers are also including more lessons on critical thinking by looking closely at the format and content of newspapers, ad-vertising, and popular culture. Here are some media literacy activities that fea-ture critical thinking based on television sources.

One way to introduce students to critical thinking about television is to look at what other students have done as critical evaluators of television. A Cana-dian education Web site (http://www.media-awareness.ca/) contains a section called "Kid Power," which features true stories of kids who took a stand and spoke out. For instance, one "Kid Power" hero is Virginie, a teenager whose sis-ter was robbed and killed as she was walking to a relative's house after buying a loaf of bread. While experts debate the connection between TV violence and real-life murders, Virginie took action and started a petition drive. She made ap-pearances on TV, radio, and at conferences all over Canada and presented the prime minister with signatures of 1.3 million Canadians who also believed there was too much violence on TV. Teachers can have students access the "Kid Power" site or they can download and distribute copies of the two-page story to students and discuss how critical thinking led Virginie to take action on an issue she was personally involved in.

Another way to initiate critical thinking about television is to provide classification activities in which students reach some conclusions after classifying and comparing programs, as well as analyzing the content and techniques of TV.

- Teachers and students kept a list of the TV shows they watched in a week. They brainstormed categories and organized their list into sitcom, news, cartoon, soap opera, talk show, drama, and so on. They discussed the categories looking for subthemes, behaviors, formats, kinds of information, and reasons for watching different kinds of shows.

- TV shows and categories were also related to outcome questions. Which categories are we most interested in? Which ones have more violence? What emotions do different ones generate such as sadness, anger, or happiness? Which ones make us laugh the most or scare us the most? Which ones use insults, name-calling, or put-downs?

- Two local newscasts from different stations were taped and compared. Or a local newscast was compared with a national newscast. Questions that prompted some critical thinking included: Who gives the news, one person or several? Does this make a difference? What format (news, weather, sports, etc.) is usually followed? What is the content of the local news? Are there similarities and differences in the news as it is presented on two different stations? If you prefer one over the other, what are some of your reasons?

- After classifying and comparing programs, a local TV personality or producer was invited to school and students asked them to comment on some of the concerns, conclusions, and questions they had generated.

To evaluate these activities, students made lists that documented their awareness that taking an evaluative stance on TV was possible and worthwhile. Students kept lists of new vocabulary words, as well as lists of statements of conclusions, concerns, and questions. Then they wrote paragraphs and short essays on themes, for example, ways TV could be improved, the effects of TV, and what I learned about TV. The next section describes how teachers show students how to evaluate information from the World Wide Web.

Evaluating Web Pages

Today students with access to databases and networks have the same powerful information-gathering tools as adult researchers. However, the volume of Web sites in 2000 was estimated to be 3.6 million (Young, 2000). This means that students and teachers need searching strategies and that selecting the "best" Web sites is a real challenge. With no quality, taste, or reliability filter, the information seeker must learn how to evaluate coded information. For example, in a Web site address the URL extension can signal the nature of a site. Commercial businesses' URLs usually include **.com,** federal government sites end in **.gov,** K–12 schools include **k12** in the address, and college and university sites often include **.edu.** Nonprofit organizations usually include **.org,** and a site with a tilde (~) in the address usually indicates that the page is created by an individual who may not represent an organization, business, or school. In addition to knowledge of Internet codes, other tools include checklists that list questions for evaluating attributes like content, credibility, citations, copyright, and site continuity. Some current Web site evaluation tool addresses include:

> http://members.aol.com/xxmindyxx/evaluate/intro.html
>
> http://www.uwec.edu/Admin/Library/10cs.html
>
> http://www.ala.org/parentspage/greatsites/criteria.html

One way to help students become critical users of the Internet is to have them evaluate sites. In the next section I describe some lesson plans and evaluation activities from two current sites. The first one is Shrock's (1997) evaluation lessons for single web sites. The second is Valenza's (1999) evaluation lesson for multiple sites.

Evaluating A Single Web Site

When you open Shrock's 1997 Web site http://school.discovery.com/schrockguide/eval.html, you will find surveys that students complete as they look at a Web site. Part One is called "Looking at and Using the Page" (see Box 7.1). Most of the questions are followed with by the responses YES/NO. After some of the questions I have inserted my critique in square brackets. As you read you will see that the questions in Part One are mostly about the user-friendliness of the site. The accuracy of the information is not questioned, only the accuracy of the photos. Also, you will see that students are to use the yes/no responses and write a paragraph explaining why or why not they would recommend the site to a friend. You can reproduce the questions in Box 7.1 and have students use them on selected Web sites.

BOX 7.1

Part One
- Does the page take a long time to load [Note: What is long? What is short?]
- Are the pictures on the page helpful?
- Is each section of the page labeled with a heading?
- Did the author sign his/her real name?
- Did the author give you his/her E-mail address?

(continued)

BOX 7.1 CONTINUED

- Is there a date on the page that tells you when it was last updated?
- Is there an image map (big picture with links) on the page?
- Is there a table (columns of text) on the page? [Note: What is source code?]
- If so, is the table readable with your browser? [Note: What is the source code?]
- If you go to another page on the site, can you get back to the main page?
- Are there photographs on the page?
- If so, can you be sure that the photographs have not been changed by the author?
- If you're not sure, should you accept the photos as true?

Aha, now we are beginning to think critically

Part Two is "What's on the Page and Who Put It There?" (See Box 7.2) Again, like Part One, the responses YES/NO are at the end of each question. Part Two starts to get at critical thinking by asking students to give their opinions about the information they find. At the end, the students are directed to look at their responses, write their opinion of the content, and describe how they are going to use the Web site.

BOX 7.2

Part Two
- Does the title of the page tell you what it is about?
- Is there a paragraph on the page explaining what it is about?
- Is the information on the page useful for your project?
- If not, what can you do next? _____
- Would you have gotten more information from an encyclopedia? [Would we have to look at an encyclopedia?]
- Is the information on the page current? [How would this be determined—by a date?]
- Does up-to-date information make a difference for your project? [A good question]
- Does the page link you to some other good information?
- Does the author of the page present some information that you disagree with?
- Does the author of the page present some information that you think is wrong?
- Does some information contradict information you found elsewhere?
- Does the author use absolute words (like *always* or *never*)?
- Does the author use superlative words (like *best* or *worst*)?
- Does the author tell you about him- or herself?
- Do you feel the author is knowledgeable about the topic?
- Are you positive the information is true?
- What can you do to prove the information is true?

All together, Shrock's questions appear to be good checklists for introducing novice researchers to evaluation of single Web sites. However, because the Internet is a system of multiple Web sites loaded with unfiltered and often contradictory information, the evaluation process should be conducted on multiple Web sites.

Evaluating Multiple Web Sites

Joyce Valenza's WebQuest (1999; http://mciu.org/~spjvweb/evalwebteach.html) provides lesson plans that include an evaluation chart that students complete as they look at up to five sites that deal with the same topic. Valenza cautions that students in elementary and middle school should examine age-appropriate sites, and I suggest that three sites on the same topic might be enough for novice evaluators. Box 7.3 contains a modified version of some of the procedures that Valenza suggests teachers follow.

BOX 7.3

Lesson Overview
This lesson works well when a content teacher and a library information specialist collaborate early in the school year to give students a baseline for evaluating Web sites they will be using as they do research throughout the school year. One class session can be used but several sessions may be required for students to gain full benefit of thinking critically about information sources. Here is how one 60-minute session might work. First, students spend about 40 minutes working in groups of four to examine and evaluate Web sites relating to a particular topic. All of the groups examine the same set of Web pages. Each student assumes a particular role. One checks site content, another checks on credibility/authority, while other individuals rate bias/purpose and usability/design. For the last 20 minutes of the session the teacher and the librarian lead a discussion to summarize the strengths and weaknesses of each site and try to reach consensus on which were the best sites.

Resources and Web Sites
One workstation per student is ideal, but a lab situation with at least one station for each small group of 4 students will work. Each student will need a copy of an evaluation chart.

Web Site Chart

    Evaluator role: _____Content _____Credibility _____Bias _____Usability

	Site Name/URL	Strengths	Weaknesses	Rank
Site 1_____	/ URL _____			
Site 2_____	/ URL _____			
Site 3_____	/ URL _____			

(continued)

BOX 7.3   CONTINUED

Three to five Web sites are selected on the basis of accessibility and appropriateness for students. For example, smoking is a controversial issue and there are several sites to choose from for a site evaluation lesson.

- Smoking and Cancer (http://www.oncolink.com/causeprevent/smoking/)
- Smoking Use among Teens (http://informatics.dent.umich.edu/health/service/teensmoking/index.html)
- Tobacco Industry Information (http://www.gate.net/~jcannon/tobacco.html)
- American Lung Association (Tobacco Control) (http://www,lungusa.org/)

Procedures
Tell students they are to each assume a particular specialist role within their group and give each student a list of the following questions and a copy of the evaluation chart.

1. *Content* Specialist questions:
   - Does the site cover the topic comprehensively and accurately?
   - Is the information understandable? Is it too hard or too simple?
   - Is this site unique? Does it offer something the others do not?
   - Are the links well chosen and sufficient?
   - Is the information current? When was the site created? What is the publication date? When was it last revised? Do the dates make a difference for this particular topic and subject matter?
   - Would a book or encyclopedia give you better information?
   - Would you include this site in your bibliography?

2. *Credibility/Authority* Specialist questions:
   - Who is responsible for this site?
   - What are their credentials?
   - Have the authors cited their own sources?
   - What is the domain name? Is the end.com,.gov,.edu and is this a clue? (.com is a commercial site,.gov is government,.edu is a university)
   - Would you include this site in your bibliography?

3. *Bias/Purpose* Specialist questions:
   - Why does this site exist? Is it a personal, commercial, government, or organizational site?
   - Do you detect any bias? Is it one-sided? Is there a hidden message? Is it trying to persuade you to change your mind? Is the bias useful to you?
   - Can you tell facts from opinions?
   - Would you include this site in your bibliography?

4. *Usability/Design* Specialist questions:
   - Is the site easy to navigate? Is it user-friendly?
   - Is there a well-labeled content area?
   - Do the graphics, art, buttons, etc. enhance the message?
   - Is there consistency in the formatting of each page?

BOX 7.3 CONTINUED

- Do the pages appear clean, uncluttered?
- Do the links work?
- Would you include this site in your bibliography?

Small Group Directions
Groups should all look at the same sites while the students focus their attention on their specialist roles. At the end of the individual evaluation time (approximately 40 of the 60 minutes), direct each group to spend about 5 minutes sharing its individual ratings and reaching some consensus. Ask them to rank the sites with one being the best and so on, or ask them to simply decide which one was the best and which one was the worst.

Whole Class Discussion
Call the whole class together and create a display with a column for recording each of the rankings from the small groups. Using a flip chart, an overhead projector, or dry erase board, record the titles of the Web pages so each group can display its rankings. The following array is one way to look for patterns and correlations across the groups.

	Rankings		
Class Groups	*Site 1*	*Site 2*	*Site 3*
A	1	2	3
B	2	1	3
C	1	2	3
D	2	1	3
E	1	3	2
F	2	1	3
Sum of Ranks	9	10	17

Sum the rankings for each site to find the one with the lowest total. In this example Site 1 scores 9, Site 2 scores 10, and Site 3 scores 17. The consensus of the class is that Sites 1 and 2 are clearly better than Site 3. Discuss the results to confirm whether or not the highly ranked sites are the ones to use in research projects. Ask other evaluation questions such as: What factors affect the decision to use or ignore different sites? Could the lowest ranked site still contain special or valuable information even though it was ranked last?

Web Site Apprentices

The two Web site evaluation lessons that we have just read are typical kinds of school lessons in which students learn *about* something as observers. In these lessons the teachers selected the Web sites and supplied the questions. This is a common and useful practice but it is different than the situation in which students learn by constructing their own Web sites at school. The next section describes how students and teachers at Unity Point School in Carbondale, Illinois, constructed a Web site to document the environmental work they do in the school's on-site outdoor education lab. The students and teachers at the school create and use Web pages in language arts, science, and social studies classes to document, evaluate, and disseminate information. The information in this Web site was generated by the students and teachers who worked outdoors for one week in June 1999. They studied and planned, planted grass, flowers, trees, and constructed a bridge over a wetland, for about four hours each day. Then the sixth-grade students and teachers worked inside about two hours each day and created a Web page with this address:

http://www.up140.jacksn.k12.il.us/habitat/index.html

The Web site development was part of a Goals 2000 grant and features pictures with captions of the various outdoor lab activities such as building planters and construction of the foot bridge. The teachers and students used FrontPage 2000, a software package for designing and publishing Web sites. Their home page has links to: a mission statement for the outdoor lab, how the outdoor lab activities meet Illinois Learning Standards, and photos and captions that document lab activities including composting, bridge construction, water planting, the plant garden, and the trees that students have planted.

Sarah, a seventh grade-student was one of the Web page writers. She showed me the trees link that contained pictures and the following text:

> In the past spring of 1999, the kindergarten planted four Red Oaks. During the summer, on June 16, 1999, five Cypress trees were planted at the east pond. The Cypress trees will be moved to the future deep pond later on. At the southwest end of the property about 100 trees were planted. The types included: Gray Dogwood, Nutall Oak, Silky Dogwood, Pecan, Persimmon, Shumard Oak, Cherrybark Oak, and Overcup Oak. Sticks were placed by the seeds so their location can be easily identified.

Sarah told how they verified the information and checked on the accuracy of tree names by consulting with the middle-school science teacher who used his knowledge and his tree books as references. Sarah reported that the school has a technical support person who provided guidance and troubleshooting that enabled them to publish their pictures, captions, and text for the Web site. Creating a Web site involved following complex directions, posing and answering hundreds of questions, and making hundreds of decisions related to content, purpose, accuracy, and usefulness.

Sarah's applied literacy work in Web site construction points out a crucial difference between *doing* evaluation using someone else's questions and *being* an evaluator whose questions emerge from a desire to complete a challenging and satisfying task. The assumption in the apprenticeship model is that, because you want to be someone who, in this case, can construct a Web page, you essentially teach yourself. Of course this assumption means that not everyone will learn equally well. Sometimes we find it difficult or impossible to learn the specific tasks that go with specific roles so we drop out, change our direction, or do something else. This was not the case for Sarah and her classmates. They successfully constructed a Web site because they had some prerequisite computer skills, they had help from a school-based technical support professional, and they worked publicly with other students and teachers.

New Literacy and Web Site Construction

The reading and thinking and decision making that students use to construct a Web site is technical, multimodal, and highly collaborative. Instead of reading a page of print with an occasional picture or illustration by oneself, the students must understand a mix of words and images as they move back and forth between the computer screen and the set of directions, all the while consulting and checking with each other. This setting requires an active and open type of "shared literacy" in which understandings, decisions, questions, and meanings are negotiated publicly in order to complete the larger task. The sixth graders are involved in what is called the "new literacy" where as adults there is a good chance they will work in a setting where there will be data processing equipment, lots of information, and a premium will be "placed on analyzing and translating that information" [and workers will need to know] "how to observe, how to use group discussion to solve problems, and how to translate data into different representations, from, say, lists to visual charts" (Myers, 1996, p. 12).

Because Sarah and her classmates are already doing this in sixth grade they are learning lifelong information-evaluation strategies. In this setting, the students and the teachers are active decision makers who read, think, talk, listen, and decide with equal persuasive power. This is precisely what is happening in the workplaces that many students will encounter as adults.

In order to get a closer look at how evaluation was built into the task of creating a Web site we will study a portion of a set of simplified directions for constructing a Web site using FrontPage 2000. The school technical support person prepared a simplified set of instructions so that students could successfully navigate the maze of text, icons, and visual arrays that accompany the FrontPage 2000 software. In the last section of the handout To Insert Shared Borders, there are at least ten subtasks that are handled by a group of students and teachers. I've numbered the separate directions, choices, and decisions. As you read this you should realize that this is only a small subset of tasks. The entire set of directions involves hundreds of questions and decisions that are required to get raw information into cyberspace.

1. **Direction.** Click [Format] in your menu bar. A dialog box will appear.
2. **Choices.**   Select whether you want borders on all pages or on the current page.
3. **Decision.**   All pages or just current page?
4. **Direction.** Select type of border.
5. **Choices.**   Top, left, right, bottom?
6. **Decision.**   If you select top or left border, you can include navigational bars.
7. **Direction.** Navigational bars?
8. **Choices.**   Navigational bars allow the user to connect to the other pages in your Web. These are also known as "hyperlinks."
9. **Direction.** Click [OK] when you are finished.
10. **Choices.**   Are we finished?

Constructing is Evaluating

When students construct a Web site, they automatically have a purpose, are concerned about content, are aware of the credibility of their information, and the usability of the site. Evaluation criteria are built into the task as they look at the screen images, check the directions on the handout, scroll, select, click on menu bars, highlight, cut and paste, and position pictures and text. The students have a vision of a product that contains the contents they have created; they have personal interest and ownership; and, as they package the information for others, they make hundreds of evaluative decisions. In addition to the built-in critical thinking that takes place during the initial work on the Web site, evaluation is not just a one-shot activity; it is ongoing. Because the outdoor education lab is an ongoing learning site for students from grades k-8, the Web site will be continually upgraded, changed, revised, and evaluated. The continual development of the site by students provides a natural setting where evaluation is continuous and built-in to the use and refinement of a site that displays their work to others from around the world! Knowing that their Web site is subject to worldwide peer review is a powerful incentive for students at Unity Point School to be critical of their work. So questions about the content, credibility, bias/purpose, and usability of the site (from the preceding lesson plan in Valenza's WebQuest site) become personalized and second nature because the students care.

Summary

In several vignettes in this chapter teachers cautioned middle-grade students that, even though information is packaged very attractively and delivered effortlessly today, they have to be wary of myth and misinformation. Other vignettes, lesson plans, and examples in this chapter illustrated how teachers provide middle-grade students with thinking tools for evaluating information and information sources. Two perspectives were provided.

In the first part of the chapter students were critical observers who subjected single and multiple sources of information to explicitly sequenced questions. They "learn" that questions are the tools we use in order to judge the credibility, purpose, relevance, and usefulness of information. In the second part the students were apprentices who processed hundreds of questions and decisions as they constructed a Web site to document and disseminate what they learned in their school outdoor environmental lab. In this project, the teachers and students did not have an explicit sequence of questions. Instead they negotiated their way through a maze of directions, choices, and decisions to produce a product from raw information they created.

It is important to keep in mind that both approaches are needed. School situations, teacher expertise, and student circumstances vary greatly and often dictate which approaches to evaluation are possible. When we consider that research strongly suggests that humans find it easier to believe than disbelieve, and middle-grade and high school students often use only the first source they encounter, the job of guiding students to evaluate information more carefully is, indeed, a formidable task.

While an increasing number of teachers can arrange applied literacy activities in which students use evaluation tools to produce new information, others present literacy lessons in which students practice evaluating someone else's information using lists of questions. Both approaches represent the kinds of alternatives middle-grade teachers need in order to equip students with evaluation tools they'll need to function successfully in the information age.

Finally, evaluating information sources is a big topic on the Internet. I asked teachers and students to name favorite sites. I have located, looked at, and evaluated some myself. I have also found some that teachers describe in journal articles. One person suggested that I list the top twenty sites, but that is impossible given that there are almost four million different Web sites out there. Instead, I've listed some in Appendices C and D that are being used, have been reviewed, and are reported to be especially worthwhile inquiry sources and tools.

References

Baines, F. (1995). *Castles*. New York: Franklin Watts.

Bass, H. J. (1991). *People in time and place: Our country*. Morristown, NJ: Silver Burdett & Ginn.

Bower, B. (1991). True believers. *Science news, 139*, 14–15.

Douglas, N. L., & Dobos, C. (2000). Introducing students to the critical reading of textbooks. *Michigan Reading Journal, 32*(1), 22–27.

FrontPage 2000 [Computer software]. (1999). Microsoft Corporation.

Gilbert, D. T. (1991, February). How mental systems believe. *American psychologist, 46*(2), 107–119.

Guy, C. L., & Wasserstein, P. (1996, February 4). *The marriage of instruction and evaluation.* Paper presented at Colorado Council IRA meeting in Denver.

Ignatieff, M. (1997, March). The elusive goal of war trials. *Harper's Magazine, 294,* 15–18.

Kubey, R., & Baker, F. (1999, October, 27). Has media literacy found a curricular foothold? *Education Week, 19*(9), 38, 56.

Myers, M. (1996). *Changing our minds. Negotiating English and literacy.* Urbana, IL: National Council of Teachers of English.

Norris, S. P., & Ennis, R. H. (1989). *Evaluating critical thinking.* Pacific Grove, CA: Midwest.

Patterson, F., Patterson, J., Hunnicutt, C. W., Grambs, J. D., & Smith, J. A. (1967). *This is our land* (2nd ed.). Syracuse, NY: Random House.

Perin, D. (1998). [Review of the book Changing Literacies]. *Journal of Adolescent & Adult Literacy, 42*(1), 68–70.

Ramachandran, V. S., & Blakeslee, S. (1998). *Phantoms in the brain.* New York: William Morrow.

Shrock, K. (1997). *Kathy Shrock's guide for educators: Critical evaluation of a website.* On-line. Available at: http://school.discovery.com/schrockguide/eval.html

Stahl, S. A., Hynd, C. R., Britton, B. K., McNish, M. M., & Bosquet, D. (1996). What happens when students read multiple documents in history? *Reading Research Quarterly, 31*(4), 430–456.

Valenza, J. (1999). *Evaluating web pages: A webquest.* On-line. Available at: http://mciu.org/~spjvweb/evalwebteach.html

Vansledright, B. A., & Kelly, C. (1998, January). Reading American history: The influence of multiple sources on six fifth graders. *Elementary School Journal, 98*(3), 239–266.

Young, T. E., Jr. (2000). Networth. *Knowledge Quest, 29*(2), 44–45.

8

Applied Literacy Minilessons

Teachers would be better off to regard their role as journeyman readers working with knowledgeable and purposeful apprentices rather than purveyors of truth.

Pearson, et al., 1990

Minilessons are an important instructional component of the applied literacy activities presented in this book. Explicit modeling by the teacher can take place at different times within the larger context of a thematic unit. For example, if the teacher notices that the texts and sources contain unfamiliar vocabulary, a minilesson on words and concepts can be presented before and during the time students are reading and searching for information. Or, if students need help finding answers to their questions, the teacher can provide a minilesson on question–answer relationships to model how to find and/or construct answers from different sources. Some minilessons are taught spontaneously in response to an observed need, while others are planned in advance because the teacher anticipates some reading and writing problems that novice researchers will encounter. Minilessons are teacher-directed activities that focus on one learning strategy. They last from five to twenty minutes and consist of an introduction and teacher modeling, student modeling, a summary and reflection, and a follow-up when students practice the strategy and to find out if it helped them.

Middle-grade students are in transition from learning how to read to using reading to learn. Although they are enthusiastic, curious, and energetic about the world around them, they are novices at learning from content area and informational text. They are not fully ready to conduct research on their own. Minilessons are one kind of scaffolded activity that will guide and support them as they go from crawling to walking upright.

In this chapter, I describe how teachers are prepared to conduct minilessons that model information-seeking strategies at the time they are needed, using the information sources that the students are using. When a minilesson is conducted near to or at the same time the student problem occurs, and when the teacher models the strategy using the sources the students are using, the chances that the strategy will be practiced immediately and used by the students increases. Of course, it is not always possible to teach at exactly the right time and in the right place in the material, but the closer to the "teachable moment" the better. The following vignette provides an example of a minilesson on inferencing.

Vignette

"Mrs. Lynn, We're not sure why they say this sunflower is valuable." Rhonda and her team of three seventh-grade students were doing research on endangered plants as part of an ecology unit in science in Ruth Lynn's classroom. This was the second day in a row that students had asked her for help in understanding some of the books, so she decided to do a comprehension minilesson on inferencing the next day.

When the class settled down Ruth said, "I know that sometimes the information you are looking for is hard to find in some of our sources, so I want to show you how to think so that you can get full understanding of the text. The kind of thinking I am talking about is inferencing. She wrote the word on the chalkboard and said, "In order to fully understand written material we always do some inference thinking. We all infer while we read no matter how easy or how hard a text is or how much of our memory we need to use. Inference demands are made on us no matter what material we read. We do not process words as much as raise propositions about the text. For example, if we read the sentence "Joan's daughter, Sally, is an intelligent girl," we raise at least six propositions. Joan is a woman. She is a mother. Sally is younger than Joan. Sally is smart. Joan may be smart, too. Joan is proud of Sally.

Then Ruth said, "Let's try to use inferencing on these sentences. Notice that, as we read, we modify our propositions as we gather more information from the text. Listen as I read each sentence. After each one I will ask you to tell me what is being inferred so far." Ruth wants to the students to see how new information can alter and confirm earlier inferences. She wants to show them that inferencing is natural, fun, and involves predicting, taking risks, and rethinking earlier ideas. Here are the sentences she read.

John was on his way to school.
[The students inferred that John could be a student, a teacher, a substitute teacher, a principal, and maybe a parent]
He was very worried about the math lesson.
[The class inferred John was probably a student or a substitute teacher]
He thought he might not be able to control the class again today.

[The class inferred it had to be a teacher, a new teacher, a substitute teacher, or a student teacher]

He thought it was unfair for the teacher to make him supervise the class for a second time.

[The class inferred it had to be a student teacher]

After all, it was not a normal part of a janitor's duty.

[The class laughed at the surprise. The teacher laughed, too, and commented how jokes are funny when unexpected information plays a trick on our thinking.]

Ruth then said, "Let's try this on the sunflower paragraph." She passed out copies of a text on flowers to the class. This was the text that Rhonda and her team had been reading when they told Ruth they weren't sure why the flower was valuable.

> The serpentine sunflower is extremely valuable. Its seeds contain the highest level of linoleic acid of any sunflower. Vegetable oils high in linoleic acid are low in saturated fats, which are believed to contribute to heart disease. If serpentine sunflowers were bred with other sunflowers, the saturated fat content might be lower in the oil from the new flowers produced. This could lead to important health benefits (E. Landau (1992). Endangered plants. New York: Franklin Watts, p. 31).

They read the text one sentence at a time and Ruth helped them put together the following sequence of inferences:

- Serpentine sunflower seeds are high in linoleic acid.
- Vegetable oils come from seeds. [This was not stated in the text.]
- If vegetable oils from serpentine sunflower seeds are high in linoleic acid, they must be low in saturated fats.
- Saturated fats contribute to heart disease.
- Serpentine sunflower seeds are low in saturated fats, so they might not contribute to heart disease.
- We could try to make vegetable oil out of serpentine sunflower seeds.
- We could breed serpentine sunflower with other sunflowers to make a new seed that is lower in saturated fats.
- We have not done this yet, so we do not know for sure whether cross-breeding will lower the levels of saturated fat in sunflower seeds.

Ruth and the students looked back at the inferences they had made. They discussed how the value of this specific sunflower is based on a sequence of inferences. They had to link the high level of linoleic acid to the low level of saturated fat. They had to supply the missing information that vegetable oil comes from plant seeds. They had to link the low level of saturated fat to heart disease. The value of this flower is also linked with a big *IF.* They had to infer that this flower may lead to the development of a new flower that yields a new sunflower oil low in saturated fats that would sell well because it would not contribute to heart disease as much as some other oils. They inferred that this was not yet a fact but only an idea that might result in this sunflower becoming more valuable. This leads to the conclusion that we ought to protect this plant for its potential to help us produce vegetable oils low in saturated fats that might lower heart disease.

In this minilesson on inferencing Ruth followed principles of direct teaching (see Carnine, Silbert, & Kameenvi, 1997; Duffy et al., 1987). First, she let students know what they were going to learn and she related it to their concern about understanding science sources. Second, she provided teacher modeling with the sentences about John, the janitor who was asked to supervise the math class. Third, she provided some guided practice and let students model inferencing with a passage on vegetable oil and heart disease. Fourth, she helped them summarize and reflect on what they had been practicing and how they would use inferencing in other situations.

Ruth plans to follow up this lesson with independent practice and application opportunities for students. She knows students will encounter future sources that require inferencing and she will be ready to prompt them to think about the examples and the thinking that occurred in this minilesson. She is prepared to help students use their inference strategies with future texts that push them to infer, link ideas, raise propositions, and draw conclusions.

So Many Strategies, So Little Time

Over the past two decades a host of excellent content literacy teaching strategies were invented by researchers and teachers to help students comprehend and learn from text. For example, Tierney, Readence, and Dishner's 1995 compendium, *Reading Strategies and Practices,* the fourth edition, contains over eighty teaching ideas, seventeen more than the preceding edition. A check of the table of contents for strategies that are directly related to teaching information literacy reveals seven strategies for teaching vocabulary, eight for studying, ten for integrating reading, writing, and content areas, and twelve for developing comprehension and critical thinking. How many strategies do you think you need to help your students learn from text? Are thirty-seven teaching ideas enough or do you want some more? When I think about this I am reminded of a successful high school wrestling coach who believed that a novice wrestler was better off mastering four or five moves that fit his particular speed, strength, and style than trying to learn as many as ten or twenty.

In this chapter, the same philosophy is followed. Instead of describing many strategies I have decided to focus on strategies that are especially applicable to middle-grade teaching situations. My reason for this approach is the reality that, unless there is some immediate payoff for teachers and students, content literacy strategies will be resisted, ignored, or discredited. The truth is that, generally speaking, content literacy teaching strategies are not part of the culture of teaching content subjects (Alvermann, 1986; O'Brien, Stewart, Moje, 1995). Many remain hidden in the pages of education journals and college textbooks, some are tried one time, live for a few days, and die out because there was no apparent payoff for either the teacher or the student. When a strategy becomes alive it is because a teacher modeled it effectively, the students used it repeatedly, it met an immediate student need, and there was evidence that it made a difference—the payoff was obvious.

Minilesson Formats

Minilessons focus on one strategy, and sometimes they are repeated, depending on how students respond, or they are discontinued when different modeling is needed. Like the minilesson in the opening vignette, there are four parts plus a follow-up. The first four parts are intended to last no more than twenty minutes. The follow-up activities usually take place over several days or more.

1. *Introduction:* The teacher lets the students know what they are going to learn and relates the lesson to what they are doing at that time in the classroom. In the vignette about inferencing, Ruth defined inferencing and related it to the comprehension problems the students were experiencing.

2. *Teacher modeling:* The teacher presents the students with a concrete example and application of the strategy. The teacher uses an authentic source from the current theme or unit of study and draws the students into a discussion of how they use the strategy as they search for information. In the vignette, Ruth modeled inferencing with the class using the paragraph on John, the surprise janitor who was helping teach math.

3. *Student modeling:* This activity flows from the previous step and uses authentic sources. The teacher gradually shifts the responsibility to the students and lets them go ahead on their own, providing feedback on how they are doing. The teacher makes sure the students are using the strategy before they are allowed to practice it on their own. This step features teacher and student interaction and flows so smoothly from the teacher modeling that it almost seems like one step. In the vignette, Ruth helped the students as they made inferences using the sunflower paragraph.

4. *Summarizing and reflecting:* The teacher asks students what they have learned and how they will use it to comprehend sources: How do we make inferences? What information did we use that was not in the text? How might we use this in future reading and thinking activities? In the minilesson, Ruth and the students discussed their list of inferences, which led them to some conclusions about the potential value of a new sunflower oil that was low in saturated fat.

Follow-up activities after the minilesson provide opportunities for students to practice, apply the strategy to new material, and think about how the strategy helped them. The teacher provides plenty of encouragement and helps them see their own progress and improvement in using the strategy successfully.

Vocabulary Minilessons

Effective vocabulary lessons provide both immediate and long-range help, especially in content area subjects that feature special vocabulary. Having a full and precise understanding of the meanings of words not only plays a crucial role in reading comprehension, it also is crucial to other aspects of communication, including writing, speaking, and listening (Johnson, 2001). There is a body of research indicating that, when the following six factors are present, vocabulary lessons help students comprehend texts (Nagy & Herman, 1987; Wixson, 1986).

1. Teach only the words that are important to the central content of the information.
2. Teach the words in a context that is relevant to the text being read.
3. Relate the words to the students' prior knowledge.
4. Group the words in topical or semantic categories and relate the categories to the students' experiences.
5. Expose the words to the students in a variety of reading and writing situations.
6. Use plenty of class discussion and make the students use the words in their writing.

These factors will be illustrated in the following sample minilessons. The first one features the concept of definition strategy or word map, and the second one illustrates semantic mapping. These powerful strategies promote student independence, they work well with expository text, and can be taught before, during, or after reading (Cooper, 1993).

Word Maps

This activity is not a one-shot lesson and usually must be practiced and used three or four times over a period of several weeks in order to be meaningful for students. In the following example, the introduction and teacher modeling would take one fifteen-minute minilesson. The student modeling and reflection would make up a second minilesson. Further student modeling and independent applications would be conducted in the third and fourth minilessons.

Introduction: First the teacher presents a word map of a familiar word to show the students the kinds of information that go into a definition (Figure 8.1).

What is it?

The way people are ruled is called:

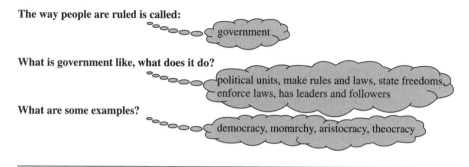

government

What is government like, what does it do?

political units, make rules and laws, state freedoms, enforce laws, has leaders and followers

What are some examples?

democracy, monarchy, aristocracy, theocracy

FIGURE 8.1

The teacher goes over the map with the students and tells them, "When we really know a word we can tell what it is (the larger category it fits under), what it is like (its parts or purpose, how it's used), and identify some examples (and, often, nonexamples)." The teacher and students can discuss the differences between the examples. Democracies have leaders elected openly by the people, monarchies have leaders (kings, queens) who are family members of the ruling class of people, aristocracies have leaders who are the richest people, and theocracies are ruled by religious leaders. Next the teacher and the class construct a definition of *government* (write sentences) using the map. One example might be: *A government is an organization that determines the way groups of people make laws, rules, and select leaders.*

Teacher modeling: Next the teacher gives the students a concrete example and application of the strategy and uses an authentic source from the current theme or unit of study, drawing them into a discussion of how they use the strategy as they search for information. Here is a passage from an expository text about an early ecologist, Aldo Leopold.

> Complex relationships among different species kept a natural community healthy. On the mountain, deer provided food for wolves and the wolves kept the deer population down. As long as there weren't too many deer browsing the hillsides, trees and shrubs would flourish. These trees and shrubs held the soil in place which, in turn, enabled grasses to grow and helped prevent erosion. "Ecology" was a term that scientists were just beginning to use for the study of community interactions such as these (Anderson, 1995, p. 45).

The teacher and students read this together and, with help from the teacher, the class completes a word map for *ecology* (Figure 8.2).

What is it?

Scientific study of interactions and relationships among animals, plants, and living things in natural settings

What is it like?

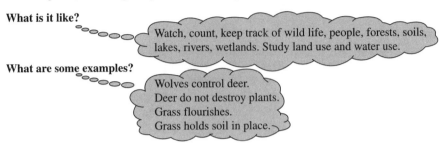

Watch, count, keep track of wild life, people, forests, soils, lakes, rivers, wetlands. Study land use and water use.

What are some examples?

Wolves control deer.
Deer do not destroy plants.
Grass flourishes.
Grass holds soil in place.

FIGURE 8.2

Student modeling: This activity flows from the previous step and uses authentic sources. The teacher gradually shifts the responsibility to the students and lets them go ahead on their own by having them work in teams to complete a comparative word map for three kinds of wetlands: marsh, swamp, bog. The teacher supplies the map framework and the students fill in the details using their science text, their prior knowledge, and an easy nonfiction text on wetlands (Fowler, 1998).

What is it?

Marsh	*Swamp*	*Bog*
What is it like?	*What is it like?*	*What is it like?*
The ground is under water most of the time. It is too wet for trees and shrubs to take root. Cattails and reeds grow in marshes. Located near lakes.	Ground is flooded part of the time. Some trees and shrubs can grow in swamps. Water comes from rivers, streams, and lakes.	Ground is damp and spongy. Water comes from rain, not a stream or lake. Plant life is very simple. Moss covers the ground and trees and shrubs grow.
Examples	*Examples*	*Examples*
Areas of Crab Orchard Refuge; Jackson and Union County in Illinois*	Everglades in Florida*	Dolly Sods in West Virginia*

*These examples are from the text author (you can supply your own).

As the students read, discuss, and complete the map the teacher provides feedback on how they are doing.

Summarizing and reflecting: The class discusses their word maps. The teacher helps them see that, although they have different features, the three kinds of wetlands share the same functions: preventing flooding during heavy periods of rain, storing water during dry spells, and serving as habitats for important plants and animals. They also discuss how word maps help us learn new words, comprehend sources, and remember and use important information

Semantic Mapping

Because words are easier to learn, remember, and use when they are related to what we already know and are presented in meaningful categories, semantic maps are a good learning/study strategy. They are often used by teachers to review concepts and ideas after the students have been reading, writing, and preparing reports. They are also used by middle-grade students as a learning/study strategy. A sample minilesson on the vocabulary associated with protective habitats will illustrate the process of semantic mapping.

Introduction: First the teacher uses a semantic map of familiar words to show the students how to categorize and arrange words in meaningful clusters. In this example the students generated a list of words in response to the question, "What are some things in or about our homes that protect us?" The words from the students include: roof, locks, smoke alarms, windows, furnaces, air conditioning, insulated walls, fences, burglar alarms, lights, window screens, telephones, basement shelter, strong walls. The teacher and the class then mapped the words into two categories based on what the items protect us from.

Homes protect us

From Weather	*From Danger/Crime*
roof	locks
windows	window screens
furnaces	smoke alarms
air conditioning	fences
insulated walls	burglar alarms
basement shelter	telephone
	strong walls

Teacher modeling: Next the teacher gives the students a concrete example and application of the strategy and uses an authentic source from the current theme or unit of study, drawing them into a discussion of how they use semantic mapping as they search for information. The class has multiple copies of three texts on castles: Baines (1995), Jessop (1993), and Macaulay (1977). To save time, the teacher directs the students to specific pages in the texts and asks them to read, review the illustrations, and list parts of a castle that protect the people living in them. After five to seven minutes, the teacher and the class work together to make a semantic map using the following terms:

Protective Parts of Castles

drawbridge	ramparts (shield)	portcullis (gate)
the keep	watch towers	moat (water)
outer wall	inner wall	spiral staircase

The words are discussed and defined and students see how the terms describe defensive barriers (*drawbridge, portcullis, moat, walls, keep*) and warning and fighting structures (*ramparts, watchtowers, spiral staircase*).

Student modeling: The teacher gradually shifts the responsibility to the students and lets them go ahead on their own by having them work in teams to complete a semantic map of features of castles (words) that protected people from pollution and poison found in bad food or bad water. Again the students are directed to specific pages and illustrations to keep the minilesson moving. Depending on which sources the groups have, the teacher helps the students construct a list of words similar to the following:

Safe Food and Water

well	cistern	beer	spring
kitchen	bread plates	pantry	
toilets	garderobes	dogs	

Summarizing and reflecting: The class discusses the map. The teacher helps them understand how mapping the words can be used to think, study, remember, and write paragraphs. The students wrote the following paragraph using their semantic map.

> Here are some things that helped people keep food and water safe in a castle. The food was cooked in a kitchen that was separate from other buildings. One book said it was separate because the kitchen had to be near the spring or well for fresh water. They also had cisterns that collect rain and held water. Another book said the water sometimes became bad so they made beer that they could store safely. Instead of plates they used dried slices of bread to hold food. They had toilets called garderobes that emptied into the moat. Dogs in the castle cleaned up scraps that fell on the floor.

Comprehension Minilessons

This section features minilessons on three comprehension strategies: question–answer relationships, summarization, and expository maps. These strategies are especially important for helping middle-grade students locate, assess, and use information that answers their questions.

While seeking information to answer questions, middle-grade students may encounter some difficulty, especially if explicit answers are not easily located. To help students overcome the tendency to say, "I can't find any answers" or "It doesn't say anything about this," a series of minilessons on question-and-answer relationships (QARs) is appropriate. The QARs strategy is from Raphael (1986). To help students decide what information is the most important for their research concerns and questions, a series of minilessons on summarization (Rinehart, 1986) can help students wade through a host of facts and details. Finally, when students gather and record ideas and answers, minilessons featuring information charts (Randall, 1996) enable students to organize sources and information related to their research questions.

Question-and-Answer Relationships

Question–answer relationships provide novice researchers with strategies for making sense of expository text that requires literal and inferential thinking. In the following minilessons the teacher shows students how they can use a strategy that features three question-and-answer relationships.

Introduction and Teacher Modeling: The teacher introduces the strategy by showing them how she uses it with a biographical text on the environmentalist, Rachel Carson (Foster, 1990). The teacher says, "When we search for information to answer questions we can look for three kinds of relationships between questions and answers. The answer may be **Right There,** you may have to **Think and Search,** or you may have to find it **On Your Own.**

To model this, the teacher has either multiple copies or has reproduced portions of *The Story of Rachel Carson.* The teacher tells the students that sometimes answers are explicitly stated in the text, and directs them to pages 21–22 to find an answer to the question, "Did Rachel Carson want pesticides banned?" The students read, and find that the text says, "she never wanted them to be banned, but she wanted the hazards of use to be considered more carefully." The teacher tells them that this is an example of how the answer to a question may be "right there" in the text.

Next, the teacher tells the class that, "Sometimes we have to 'think and search' for answers because the information is not found all in one sentence or in one place in the text. In this case we have to think about our question, search through the text, and combine ideas to create an answer. For example, the answer to the question, "Why was Rachel warned not to write *Silent Spring?*" is found by combining information from the text and the illustrations on pages 21–22. The teacher and students find that there are several parts of the text that can be used to answer the question including: her poetic writing style might not fit with scientific information, people might not buy a book on pesticides, and public opinion favored the use of pesticides.

The teacher models the third QAR by telling the students, "Sometimes the answer is not in the text and searching and combining information from the text is not helpful. In this case we are 'on our own' and we must search our own information, our own knowledge, for the answer. Of course we may not have the right knowledge, but very often we have some information and we try to use it as best we can. For example, the question "Why did her [Rachel Carson's] local community have to decide whether or not to spray the trees against insects?" does not have a direct answer in the text. Nor does the text give any information about her local community. The response that insects posed a danger to the trees has to be based on our prior knowledge that insects can harm trees. Another example is the question, "Why did a neighbor telephone Rachel and call her an alarmist just before the public meeting to vote on whether or not to spray the trees?" A number of possible answers have to be based on prior knowledge about neighbors, public meetings, speeches, and voting.

Student Modeling: The teacher shifts responsibility to the students and has them use the Right There, Think and Search, and On My Own strategies. One way to do this is in a whole-class discussion during which student answers are written on the board by the teacher and the question–answer relationships are discussed. Another way is to have the students work in pairs or trios to look for information that may answer questions. In the following example, the teacher provides them with multiple copies of the book *Castles* (Baines, 1995). She also supplies three questions to answer. The students also have to decide what is the relationship between the question and the possible answer. The questions are:

> Why were castles made stronger and stronger over time?
> What is the safest place in the castle?
> How did cannons become more and more powerful?

The teacher lets the students begin and gives them some hints about page numbers to save some time. After ten minutes, the class discusses what they found. The answer to the first question, "Why were castles made stronger and stronger over time?" is stated on page 7 (weapons for attacking castles became more and more powerful) and is an example of a *right there* relationship. The answer to the second question, "What is the safest part?" is found by combining information from the text and the illustrations on pages 13–17. The keep is the thick-walled section in the center of the castle with guard towers at the corners. It is the strongest place and the hardest to get into. This is an example of a *think and search* relationship. The third question, "How did cannons become more and more powerful?" does not have an appropriate answer in the text so it is an *on my own* situation. An appropriate response such as "they could shoot larger and heavier things to break down the walls" indicates that the students have some background knowledge about guns and warfare that can be applied to this question.

Summarizing and Reflecting: Teachers often make a wall chart or bulletin board that illustrates the three kinds of questions. *Right There* has a picture of a book. *Think and Search* shows a student's head and a book. *On My Own* shows a picture of only a student's head. Lessons using this concept are simple, they feature immediate feedback, and the teacher learns to accept diverse responses. Some teachers use four or more special minilessons to initiate students into this kind of comprehension strategy. After the initial intensive minilessons the idea is referred to whenever it is appropriate.

Summarization

The simple reason that middle-grade students are novices at summarizing expository text is that summarization is a complex process. Readers have to know how to select and delete information, condense information, and transform the information by writing (Hidi & Anderson, 1986). This involves the thinking processes of identifying a theme, sorting main ideas from details, rearranging and classifying ideas, and using words that describe classes or groups of ideas. To do all of this well, a reader must be motivated and have a good reason to summarize. I recall a sixth-grade learning disabled student I was testing who read me a story about a space station that was losing oxygen. Although his oral reading word accuracy and fluency were poor, he immediately said, "Safety," when I asked him what the story was about. He said he was very interested in science, especially rockets and astronauts. His interest and motivation prompted him to summarize the story in one perfect word.

Summarization requires a relatively high level of thinking as well as a compelling purpose. In the following lessons the assumption is that the students are engaged in seeking information and finding some answers to their own questions. Because they are reading about a topic they are interested in, the summarization lessons feature text sources that have information students want.

Introduction and Teacher Modeling: The teacher introduces the strategy by discussing how we summarize all the time in order to make sense of all the detailed information we encounter and gives the following simple example. "Instead of asking about the specific wind, temperature, sky conditions, and whether or not it is raining we usually summarize all of this by asking, 'How's the *weather?*' If we read a paragraph that talks about following speed limits, using our seat belts, and paying attention we can summarize that this is all about *safety.*" Next the teacher gives the students the following paragraph from *Sitting Bull* (Iannone, 1998), and models how to summarize the paragraph in one sentence. The students are studying Native American cultures and have already begun to search for information on topics and questions they have raised.

Soon after their arrival in what is now the province of Saskatchewan, the Sioux were approached by seven members of the NorthWest Mounted Police. Sitting Bull met with Major James M. Walsh, who told the chief that his people were welcome to stay in Canada as long as they obeyed the laws. This would mean refraining from fighting with other tribes and stealing horses. Also, because Canada did not want to have diplomatic troubles with the United States, he did not want any Indians living in Canada to return to the United States and cause trouble there. Anyone who did so would not be welcome to return to Canada (p. 76).

The teacher says, "I read through the paragraph and looked for the overall or main idea. I asked myself what is the material mainly about? And I write this information in one sentence." Here is the sentence that the teacher created to summarize the text:

The Canadian police told Sitting Bull that the Sioux were welcome in Canada if they did not fight, steal, or go back to the United States and cause trouble.

The class discusses the summary and the teacher shows them that only the important information was used and nothing was used twice.

Student Modeling: The teacher gives the students a handout on summarization based on a portion of *Endangered Plants* (Landau, 1992), pages 13–14. This portion of the text was selected because it nicely illustrates the main idea of how Native Americans lived in harmony with the environment. The teacher guides the students through the exercise one paragraph at a time. The students are asked to work in pairs to read and write summary sentences. The following example is modeled after the strategy described by Rinehart and associates (1986).

Steps for Writing a Summary

Step One: Read through each paragraph and look for the overall or main idea. What is the material mainly about? Write this information in one sentence. Here is an example:

The decline of the Catalina mahogany can be traced to the island's history. Nearly 4000 years ago, when the area was inhabited only by Indians, Catalina mahogany trees were abundant. Then in 1542, the first European explorers arrived. Following the explorers, the island served as a haven for English pirates, Yankee smugglers, and Russian fur traders. (What is this mainly about? Write one sentence here.) Possible sentence: When explorers arrived in 1542, Indians lived there and mahogany trees were abundant.

During the nineteenth century, groups of white settlers arrived on Santa Catalina. Some came seeking wealth, since gold was discovered on the island just before the California Gold Rush. Other settlers came to raise sheep, cattle, horses, and goats. To be sure there was room for the newcomers, the Native American island Indians, who had always lived in harmony with nature, were shipped to the mainland by government orders. (What is this mainly about? Write one sentence here.) Possible sentence: Settlers moved in and the Native island Indians were shipped to the mainland.

Interestingly, the arrival of goats is largely responsible for the near disappearance of the Catalina mahogany tree. The animal's overgrazing destroyed much of the island's natural vegetation. Once the plant growth protecting the soil was gone, the ground became less fertile (pp. 13–14). (What is this mainly about? Write one sentence here) Possible sentence: The settlers' goats overgrazed, the ground became less fertile, and the mahogany trees almost disappeared.

> **Step Two:** What tells or explains the overall ideas you found so far? Find the most important information that explains or tells about what you wrote in the first step. Write this down in one sentence if you are summarizing a paragraph and in one, two, three, or more if you are summarizing a group of related paragraphs. Use only as many sentences as necessary.

Here are some other possible sentences:

First paragraph:	Explorers and settlers replaced the Native American Indians on Catalina Island.
Second paragraph:	Instead of living in harmony with the island the settlers allowed their goats to destroy the natural plants.
Third paragraph:	The loss of protective plants made the ground less fertile and most mahogany trees died.

The teacher discusses the summary sentences with the students and directs them to try to write one overall sentence that summarizes all three of the separate sentences. The teacher cautions that this is difficult and often two or even three sentences are needed to write clear summaries. It depends on the amount of information and the purpose of the summary. A possible summary sentence of the entire selection is:

After the Indians were forced to leave, the mahogany trees were almost destroyed because settlers allowed their animals to overgraze.

> **Step Three:** Use the following checklist to proof your summary.
> _____ I have found the overall idea that the paragraph(s) are about.
> _____ I have found the most important information that tells more about the overall idea.

_____ I have only used information that is directly related to the overall idea.

_____ I have not used any information more than once.

Summarizing and reflecting: Follow up minilessons featuring the three-step checklist are needed to give students plenty of practice in summarizing. An enlarged version of the checklist can be posted in the classroom for reference by the teacher and students. In follow-up sessions, teachers reinforce summarization by posting examples of student summaries. In this way the cycle of modeling and practice promotes independence in student summarization.

Expository Maps

The applied literacy lessons described in this book feature activities in which students ask questions, search multiple sources, and locate useful information. Because novice researchers need assistance in organizing their sources, questions, and information, the teacher shows them how to use an expository map. The expository map is adapted from the I Chart plan by Randall (1996).

Introduction and Teacher Modeling: To introduce the plan the teacher gives each student a copy of the following guide and tells them, "When we are traveling in unfamiliar places a map that shows us where we are can help us get to where we want to go. The same idea applies to a research project. Research often takes us to unfamiliar territory where new information can confuse us and we can lose our direction. Here is a map idea that can help us see where we are, where we need to go, and whether or not we may have to revisit places, look further, or stop searching. Here is an empty map that we will use as a guide." The teacher gives a copy to each student at this part of the minilesson.

Expository Map for Organizing Notes and Writing Reports

Topic	Question 1	Question 2	Question 3	Question 4
Name of Source S-1,	S-1, Q-1	S-1, Q-2	S-1, Q-3	S-1, Q-4
S-2	S-2, Q-1	S-2, Q-2	S-2, Q-3	S-2, Q-4

The teacher reviews the cells and explains that the number of questions and sources depends on the topic, the number of people doing research, the number of questions, and the availability of sources of information. The teacher also tells them that one map can be used by a team of students so that each one can try to find information for one question, or each student can look for answers to several questions using one source. When information is found, it is written on separate sheets of paper and labeled by source and question such as S-3, Q-1. Later, students come together and place the sheets of paper in an array. In that way they keep track of which questions are being answered from one or more sources and which questions may still not have any answers. At this point, student questions are discussed and answered and the teacher hands out the following copy of a partially completed expository map that illustrates how the map works.

Expository Map for Organizing Notes and Writing Reports

Topic/Sources	Question 1	Question 2	Question 3
Insect Eating Plants	Why do they eat insects?	How do they catch insects?	Why are they endangered?
S-1	S-1, Q-1	S-1, Q-2	S-1, Q-3
Endangered Plants by E. Landau (1994).	Plants need nutrients not found in soil. When grown in fertile green house soil they stop eating insects. p. 52	Pitcher plant makes nectar that attracts insects to the sweet smell. Bristles catch and hold insects. p. 49.	Pitcher plant needs wetlands and grows in bogs. Wetlands and bogs are being drained to make farmland or grazing pastures. p. 52.
S-2	S-2, Q-1	S-2, Q-2	S-2, Q-3
Bloodthirsty Beauties in *Smithsonian Magazine,* December 1992.		Venus fly trap has trigger hairs around trap. Insect touches hair, the leaves snap shut, trapping insect inside. p. 52.	In Alabama road building, pond making, cattle pastures destroy habitat for pitcher plants. p. 56.

The teacher and students review the information and they see that some sources have lots of information that matches their questions while others have no information. The teacher briefly tells them how they could write paragraphs using the questions as headings and the information under the question as the body of the paragraph. They do not do that at this point in the lesson. Instead, they stay on the topic of organizing information from different sources.

Student Modeling: At this point the teacher passes out a partially completed practice map that lists the topic (family life in a castle), four questions, and three sources.

Topic/Sources	Question 1	Question 2	Question 3	Question 4
Family Life in a Castle	What was food and cooking like?	What did they do for entertainment?	What work did people do in a castle?	Did they have water, plumbing, bathrooms?
S-1,	S-1, Q-1	S-1, Q-2	S-1, Q-3	S-1, Q-4
Castles by F. Baines (1995).				
S-2	S-2, Q-1	S-2, Q-2	S-2, Q-3	S-2, Q-4
X-Ray PIcture Book of Big Buildings of the Ancient World by J. Jessop (1993).				
S-3	S-3, Q-1	S-3, Q-2	S-3, Q-3	S-3, Q-4
Castle by David Macaulay (1977).				

Copies of the three text sources are available for the teacher to refer to and show the students where the information came from. On a separate sheet of paper the teacher has reproduced several sets of information and labeled them S-1, S-2, or S-3 to show which sources they are from. The students are told to work in pairs, examine the information, and place it on the expository map where it matches a question. They have scissors if they need to cut the sentences apart to place them on the map.

S-1   The kitchen was a separate building.
Bread, beer, wine made in the kitchen.
Large pieces of stale bread were used as plates.
There were no forks. Beer was used if the water was bad.
Dogs cleaned up scraps of food that fell on floor.

S-1   Jugglers and acrobats performed.
             Minstrels sang and mummers put on plays.
             Jesters made people laugh with funny dancing and stories.
             The lord of the castle hunted for sport.

S-1   Water came from well in kitchen. Water was sometimes bad so they made beer.

S-2   Meals and feasts were served in the great hall.
             Latrines emptied into the moat.
             Butlers and pantlers bought and stored food.
             Stewards and clerks kept records, paid the bills.
             A bailiff and reeve collected rent. Knights and archers defended the castle.
             Spring-fed well was fresh water supply.
             There were gardens, beehives, animals for meat, chickens and doves for meat and
             eggs.

S-3   Toilets called garderobes were located in the castle walls.
             Cisterns held water for sinks.

As the students work together reorganizing the information, the teacher observes and provides help when they have questions and concerns. After about ten minutes, the teacher and students stop and discuss what they have completed so far. If they need more time the lesson can be carried over to another day. The table below shows a completed expository map that the teacher can share to give the students feedback and support and show them how their practice lesson was successful.

Topic/Sources	Question 1	Question 2	Question 3	Question 4
Family Life in a Castle	What was food and cooking like?	What did they do for entertainment?	What work did people do in a castle?	Did they have water, plumbing, bathrooms?
S-1,	S-1, Q-1	S-1, Q-2	S-1, Q-3	S-1, Q-4
Castles by F. Baines (1995).	Kitchen was a separate building. Bread, beer, wine made in kitchen. Stale bread used as plates. They had no forks. If water was bad beer was used. Dogs cleaned up scraps.	Jugglers and acrobats performed. Minstrels sang and mummers put on plays. Jesters made people laugh with funny dancing and stories. The lord of the castle hunted.		Water came from well inside castle Water was bad so they made beer.

(continued)

S-2	S-2, Q-1	S-2, Q-2	S-2, Q-3	S-2, Q-4
X-Ray PIcture Book of Big Buildings of the Ancient World by J. Jessop (1993).	Castle had spring-fed well for water. Gardens, beehives, animals, chickens, and doves for meat and eggs were inside walls.	Meals and feasts were served in the great hall.	Butlers and pantlers bought and stored food. Stewards and clerks kept records, paid bills. A bailiff and reeve collected rent. Knights and archers defended the castle.	Latrines emptied into the moat.

S-3	S-3, Q-1	S-3, Q-2	S-3, Q-3	S-3, Q-4
Castle by David Macaulay (1977).				Toilets called garderobes were located in walls. Cisterns held water for sinks.

Summarizing and reflecting: The class reviews the expository map and the teacher explains how a map can help keep track of information and facilitate report writing. For example, the teacher asks, "How does all of the information under the fourth question fit together? Let's try to write a paragraph together to show how our information from at least two sources answers the question." They could have written the following paragraph by "collecting" information under question four about the water and plum.

> Water was important to life in a castle so they had wells inside the walls. They also had cisterns to catch and store water for use in the sinks. They had toilets called latrines or garderobes in the walls that emptied into the moat.

The teacher can have blank expository map sheets as models for arranging information from different sources to fit with questions they have about a topic. The maps are flexible. They can function as scaffolding for both novice researchers with a few sources and questions or experienced researchers with many sources and questions.

Summary

In this chapter I have described how timely minilessons help novice researchers understand important vocabulary and concepts, comprehend difficult text, and organize and use information to answer their questions. There is little doubt that, while enthusiastic and information-hungry middle-grade students want to know about the world, their research skills are limited. The scaffolded lessons that teachers employ fill the gap between the children's enthusiasm for information and their novice research, reading, thinking, and writing skills. Students benefit from clear and straightforward lessons that are tied as closely as possible to their questions and the specific sources they are using.

The vocabulary, comprehension, and organizational strategies presented in this chapter were selected because they represent a core of basic practices that benefit novice researchers. For example, in one sixth grade class, two girls were researching the food and cooking practices of people living in castles. They read from different sources, found information, and, with the teacher's help with the expository map, they were able to organize it in a way that made writing the following paragraph on food and eating in the Middle Ages.

> In castles the food was cooked in a kitchen that was separate from other buildings. One book we read said it was separate because the kitchen had to be located near the well for water. Another book said the water sometimes became bad so they made beer to have something to drink. Instead of plates they used slices of stale bread to hold the food. Inside the castle's outer wall they had gardens, beehives, animals for meat, and chickens and doves for meat and eggs. There were dogs in the castle that cleaned up the food scraps that fell on the floor.

The model minilessons described in this chapter featured teacher and student modeling, as well as follow-up activities. This format enabled students to practice and apply the lesson to a specific product or task and increased the chances that students, as apprentice researchers, will experience an immediate payoff.

References

Alvermann, D. (1986, June 13–14). *Why teachers resist content area reading instruction.* Paper presented at fifth annual University of Wisconsin Reading Symposium, Milwaukee, WI.

Anderson, P. (1995). *Aldo Leopold, American ecologist.* New York: Franklin Watts.

Baines, F. (1995). *Castles.* New York: Franklin Watts.

Carnine, D. W., Silbert, J., & Kameenui, E. J. (1997). *Direct instruction reading* (3rd ed.). Columbus, OH: Merrill.

Cooper, J. D. (1993). *Literacy: Helping children construct meaning* (2nd ed.). Boston: Houghton Mifflin.

Duffy, J. A., Roehler, L., Sivan, E., Rackliffe, G., Book, C., Meloth, M., Vavrus, L., Wesselman, R., Putnam, J., & Bassiri, D. (1987). Effects of explaining the reasoning associated with using reading strategies. *Reading Research Quarterly, 22,* 347–368.

Foster, L. M. (1990). *The story of Rachel Carson.* Chicago: Children's Press.

Fowler, A. (1998). *Life in a wetland.* New York: Children's Press.

Hidi, S., & Anderson, V. (1986). Producing written summaries: Task demands, cognitive operations, and implications for instruction. *Review of Educational Research, 56,* 473–494.

Iannone, C. (1998). *Sitting Bull: Lakota leader.* New York: Franklin Watts.

Jessop, J. (1993). *X-Ray picture book of big buildings of the ancient world.* New York: Franklin Watts.

Johnson, D. D. (2001). *Vocabulary in the elementary and middle school.* Boston: Allyn & Bacon.

Landau, E. (1992). *Endangered plants.* New York: Franklin Watts.

Macaulay, D. (1977). *Castle.* Boston: Houghton Mifflin.

Nagy, W. E., & Herman, P. A. (1987). Breadth and depth in vocabulary knowledge: Implications for acquisition and instruction. In M. G. McKeown & M. E. Curtis (Eds.), *The nature of vocabulary acquisition* (pp. 19–35). Hillsdale, NJ: Lawrence Erlbaum.

O'Brien, D. G., Stewart, R. A., & Moje, E. B. (1995). Why content literacy is difficult to infuse into the secondary school: Complexities of curriculum, pedagogy, and school culture. *Reading Research Quarterly, 30*(3), 442–463.

Pearson, P. D., Roehler, L. R., Dole, J. A., & Duffy, G. G. (1990). *Developing expertise in reading comprehension: What should be taught? How should it be taught?* Technical Report No. 512. Champaign, IL: Center for the Study of Reading.

Randall, S. N. (1996). Informational charts: A strategy for organizing student research. *Journal of Adolescent & Adult Literacy, 39,* 536–542.

Raphael, T. E. (1986). Teaching question–answer relationships, revisited. *Reading Teacher, 39,* 516–522.

Rinehart, S., Stahl, S., & Erickson, L. G. (1986). Some effects of summarization training on reading and studying. *Reading Research Quarterly, 21*(4), 422–438.

Tierney, R. J., Readence, J. E., & Dishner, E. K. (1995). *Reading strategies and practices: A compendium* (4th ed.). Boston: Allyn & Bacon.

Wixson, K. K. (1986). Vocabulary instruction and children's comprehension of basal stories. *Reading Research Quarterly, 21,* 317–329.

9

Applied Literacy Examples in Language Arts

Zetetikos—A Greek word meaning to seek or inquire. An apt word describing the students and teachers featured in this text.

This chapter features two examples of applied literacy. The first one is from the Cherry Creek School District, in Aurora, Colorado, where teachers created a nonfiction inquiry unit called "Birds of Prey." The students study multiple sources, gather data, and write and present reports on birds like eagles, hawks, and owls. The teachers and students use detailed rubrics that tie the student products to the Colorado reading and language arts assessment goals. The second example is from the Unity Point School in Carbondale, Illinois, where two language arts teachers created a unit on Edgar Allen Poe. The students read Poe, do Web site biography research on his life, and write a Poe-like story. The unit is used with eighth-grade students and illustrates the power of combining fiction and nonfiction. The unit nicely illustrates how teachers get students engaged with high quality literature, Web site inquiry, and individual narrative writing. In both examples, students ask questions, gather data from multiple sources, produce new text, and communicate what they have learned.

Applied Writing and Speaking in Language Arts

The teachers I talked with in Denver at the 1996 Colorado International Reading Association state conference were pleased with the results of their thematic unit, Birds of Prey. They presented a session at the conference and shared a model unit in which they used fiction and nonfiction sources for teaching and assessing district language arts proficiencies in third grade. The students were excited by the topic and the language arts activities engaged virtually every student. The teachers believed the high level of motivation and effort made the unit a valid way to assess how third graders apply language arts proficiencies to acquire, organize, and share information on an interesting topic.

In order to see what it takes to help novice learners do research, I have edited the teachers' material and included more details of the portion of the unit when the students were doing research, writing reports, and presenting oral reports on self-selected birds of prey.

Although all of the examples in this book are from grades five to eight, this unit was used with third-grade students. I am including it for several reasons. First, it illustrates how much help (formats, directions, models) teachers must give to novice researchers. Second, the teaching ideas can easily be translated to higher grades. One reviewer said the example illustrated applied literacy very nicely and thought the diary format valuable for recording ideas. One middle-school teacher who read the manuscript said the teaching ideas could easily be adapted to his grade 7 and 8 language arts classes.

Birds of Prey Thematic Unit

Weeks 1–2 Understanding and Using Information

The teachers used a structured format called a "reading diary" to help students document their comprehension and reaction to reading a nonfiction book related to the birds of prey theme. The diary activity was modeled during the first two weeks of the unit by having all of the students read the nonfiction text, *Eagle Diary* (from the Endangered Animals Series, Modern Curriculum Press) and take notes in a prescribed diary with blank entry spaces. In *Eagle Diary* the main character raised a baby eagle until it was able to fly away to live in the wild. At the end of two weeks, the students used their diary entries to write a letter about how to deal with problems associated with endangered birds. This structured activity prepared them for weeks 3-6, when the students selected a particular bird of prey, gathered information, and prepared a report on their bird. Here are a few diary entry models, the letter-writing directions, and models of the student reflection and self-assessment formats.

MY DIARY	NAME _____
	SCHOOL _____
	TEACHER _____
	DATE _____

DATE _____

I would describe the main idea of this story to someone who has not read it before by saying

_____

_____

Three important events in the life of the eagle (listed in time order) are

_____

_____

_____

Page 8

DATE _____

Based on the information on pages 22 and 23, and if there were no laws to protect eagles, the following things would happen to them

_____

_____

_____

_____

Page 9

Letter Writing

The intent of this activity is to show children how they can use the new information and take some action to advocate protection for endangered species. The children are told:

Now that you have read the book and kept a diary you can use the information to write a letter. Here are some choices of letters. Select one of these or think of another one.

1. Because I want to help save our natural wildlife, I will write to the state or federal wildlife department and tell about the problems eagles have, and I will suggest how to solve the problem.
2. I will write to the wildlife department and tell them what I learned from reading this book, explain why I am concerned about eagles, and ask for additional information on how we are saving wildlife.
3. I will write to the book authors and tell them my opinion of the book. I will include my summary of what I have learned, questions I still have, and suggestions.

Student Reflections and Self-Assessment

The teachers researched their students' reactions at this point in the unit. They wanted the children to hear what others said about the project. The following items were used for student reflection.

1. I liked reading *Eagle Diary.*   Yes ___   No ___   Sometimes ___
2. It was easy to respond to the
   diary questions.   Yes ___   No ___   Sometimes ___
3. The questions were hard.   Yes ___   No ___   Sometimes ___
4. My answers were accurate
   and detailed.   Yes ___   No ___   Sometimes ___
5. I spent a lot of time thinking
   about answers.   Yes ___   No ___   Sometimes ___
6. Class discussions helped me
   answer questions.   Yes ___   No ___   Sometimes ___
7. I shared my ideas about the
   book with someone else.   Yes ___   No ___   Sometimes ___
8. I was excited by this project.   Yes ___   No ___   Sometimes ___
9. I want to learn more about
   eagles.   Yes ___   No ___   Sometimes ___
10. I like adding to and changing
    my diary entries   Yes ___   No ___   Sometimes ___

The following was used for self-assessment:

Tell how much you agree or disagree with the following thoughts about this project. If you agree a lot, mark the 5, if you agree some, mark 3, if you disagree, mark 1.

1. This project was interesting.   1   3   5
2. I learned a lot.   1   3   5
3. The questions make me think.   1   3   5
4. I used the glossary.   1   3   5
5. The map and illustrations
   helped me.   1   3   5
6. Listening and sharing during
   class discussion helped me
   understand and remember.   1   3   5
7. If I could do this project
   again I would change:
8. The most challenging part
   of the project was:
9. I did my best work on:

Weeks 3–6. Sources of Information for Individual Inquiry

At this time the unit shifted to individual inquiry and research activities and the teachers had to make sure that the children had access to sources of information that fit the theme and were appropriate for third grade. In the words of the teachers, finding selections "proved a bit challenging," but they obtained over twenty books on birds of prey at the local library. They also found the American Library Association publication, *Book Links,* to be helpful. The September 1994 issue of *Book Links* contained an annotated bibliography on owls by Mary Lou Burket. Examples of sources of other current nonfiction books on birds of prey that are excellent sources for novice researchers include:

> Arnosky, J. (1995). *All about owls.* Scholastic.
>
> Collard, S. B. (1999). *Birds of prey: A look at daytime raptors.* Franklin Watts.
>
> Jemima, P. (2000). *Eyewitness: Eagles & birds of prey.* DK Publishing.
>
> Lamm, C. D. (1996). *Screech owl at midnight hollow.* Scholastic.

Another obvious source of information on birds of prey is the Internet. For example, a search for birds of prey on DiscoverySchool.com provides access to pictures and information for novice researchers from the A-to-Z Science section. A quick look reveals excellent information on honey buzzards in Africa and ospreys and eagles in North America. The point here is that the teachers made sure they had access to inviting and informative sources of information on birds of prey so the children could self-select a bird for their research. The sources included books, encyclopedias, magazines, videos, and the Internet.

Transition to Individual Inquiry

Now the teachers and students were shifting gears from reading the same book, *Eagle Diary,* to having students work individually with self-selected sources. To motivate students and help them select a specific bird, the teachers used videos and films on birds of prey and the children responded to an informal assessment of their listening and observation skills. This informal listening activity helped the children make the transition from the emphasis on eagles to the broader topic, "Birds of Prey," and served as a practice activity to prepare them for the formal "Listening Log" activity that came later in the unit. Examples of videos available from Amazon.com include:

> *Amazing Animals Video: Birds of Prey* (1997)
>
> *The Fascinating World of Birds of Prey* (1995)

Before viewing a video the children were given the following listening organizer that used a K-W-L format.

Listening Organizer

Name _____   Date _____

Video Title _____

What do I already know about this topic?

What do I want to know?

What did I learn?

What do I still want to know?

The listening organizer was used as a basis for whole-class discussions. The questions about what they still want to know can form the basis for future inquiry. The teachers said that one good idea was to have the students record their initial ideas in pencil. Then, during and after the class discussion, they used a color pencil to add comments and new insights to the listening organizer. The teachers collected the organizers, reviewed them, and could tell what the students were interested in, what the students knew, and what they did not know. This informal assessment gave the teachers some insight into how to conduct the next part of the unit.

Expository Writing: The Birds of Prey Research Report

During weeks three to six, students prepared individual research reports on self-selected birds of prey. They used the following Birds of Prey Notebook as a guide for gathering preliminary information. The students had class time to find sources, read, and take notes and the teachers were prepared to provide help as the children looked for information.

Birds of Prey Notebook

Research Task

Using information from a variety of sources, I will research a bird of prey and prepare a written report that includes a bibliography. I will follow the Birds of Prey Table of Contents to gather preliminary information. The notebook will be turned in with the final written report. My work will reflect the research skills learned in class, the knowledge gained from the sources, and the specific language arts instruction concerning writing mechanics. My work will be judged using the attached writing rubric. My work will be done during the school day and my final report is due _____.

Table of Contents

Name of Bird _____
    Characteristics
    Eggs, Nests, and Young
    Habitat
    Food
    Unique/Interesting Information
    Comparison to Eagles

Bibliography (sample)

Books
    Zim, H. (1983). *Birds of Prey.* Chicago: Delta Press.

Encyclopedias
    Burns, S. (1991). Watchman of the night: Barn owls. *Encyclopedia Britannica, 8,* 124–127.

Magazines
    Franklin, A., & Franklin, L. (April 1990). Pesticides and raptor eggs. *National Wildlife, 4,* 12–17.

Web Sites
    DiscoverySchool.com (search for birds of prey)

Media
    "Birds of Prey." *Nova on PBS.* February 13, 1994.

Written Report Checklist of Requirements

_____ 1. My report was written in my own words. I carefully chose words that made my report original.

_____ 2. I included enough details related to my subject to teach my audience important information.

_____ 3. There were few, if any, errors in spelling or punctuation.

_____ 4. My report was logically organized in paragraphs with original topic sentences. I covered all the categories from the notebook directions and gave specific facts and information about my bird of prey.

_____ 5. My bibliography was complete and accurate. I used at least two books and one other source like an encyclopedia or a Web site.

_____ 6. My notebook showed correct note-taking procedures and each category contained three or more facts. My written comments about these facts were thoughtful, varied, and in my own words.

_____ 7. My report had a cover with a large, realistic color picture of my bird of prey in its habitat. My title was easy to read and my name was listed as the author.

_____ 8. I made a comparison between my researched bird of prey and eagles.

Writing Rubrics

The students had copies of the writing rubric provided in detail in Appendix A. The students and the teachers used the rubric to produce and evaluate the written report and scores for each of the following writing topics were derived for the report:

Ideas and Content	1	2	3	4
Organization	1	2	3	4
Word Choice	1	2	3	4
Sentence Structure	1	2	3	4
Writing Conventions	1	2	3	4

Throughout this four-week period the students needed plenty of encouragement and help to find information, take notes, and turn the notes into sentences and paragraphs that fit with the report headings of habitat, food, and so on.

Weeks 7–9.   Speaking, Listening, Presenting

During weeks seven to nine of this unit the students used the information in their written reports to prepare oral presentations and complete a listening log. The students were given checklists for both speaking and listening. The Birds of Prey Speaking Task and the Listening Log are presented in the next section.

Birds of Prey Speaking Task

Using information from my written report, I will prepare and present an oral report on my bird of prey. The student speaking rubric will help me prepare and evaluate the report. I will present on _____.

Speaking Requirements Checklist

1. Ideas and Content. I will:
   ____ keep my audience's attention and interest
   ____ use my own words
   ____ tell what I learned about my topic
   ____ include important ideas and interesting details

2. Organization. My report will include:
  ____ a strong and interesting beginning
  ____ a detailed middle part
  ____ a clear and memorable ending
  ____ ideas presented in an order that makes sense

3. Voice. I will:
  ____ speak loudly and clearly and not too fast
  ____ watch my audience to see if I need to speak slower, faster, louder, clearly
  ____ use expression so my voice sounds natural and interesting
  ____ use my style and personality to express myself

4. Nonverbal Elements. I will:
  ____ look at my audience in a natural way
  ____ use gestures, stand straight, and move naturally
  ____ use a visual aid that will make my report clear and interesting

Speaking Rubric and Listening Log

The students had copies of the speaking and listening rubrics that are included in Appendix A. They also had a Listening Log to teach and assess listening skills that will be used when they listen to each other's reports. The students and the teachers used the following formats to evaluate the oral reports as well as their listening skills.

Speaking Rubric Scores

Ideas and Content	1	2	3	4
Organization	1	2	3	4
Voice	1	2	3	4
Nonverbal Elements	1	2	3	4

Listening Log

Directions: Complete a response sheet for each presentation you listen to. Jot down your questions, thoughts, and insights. After all the reports are given, the logs will be collected and used to assess the generic listening rubric.

Speaker _____ Date _____

Topic _____

Main Idea

Interesting Details

Comparison: The speaker's topic and my topic are alike and different.
Alike: Different:
My questions and responses and thoughts are:

    This example illustrates the kinds of directions and formats that the teachers used to help students use their reading, writing, speaking, and listening abilities to complete an inquiry project on an interesting nonfiction topic. In 2001 I talked to one of the teachers who authored the Birds of Prey unit. She said they have been using it successfully for several years, have added some new sources, and have had to redo all of the materials several times because "The children love this approach and we've had to replace the worn-out booklets and formats several times."

Inquiry and Narrative Writing in Language Arts

At Unity Point School in Carbondale, Illinois, Deanna Diel, the literature teacher, and Mike Wright, the English teacher, deliver a two-week unit on Edgar Allen Poe. Diel teaches the eighth graders about the elements of Poe's writing. Wright guides students when they do biographical research on Poe and when they write an essay on Poe and narratives using Poe's writing style. Students study Poe's writing, do biographical research on Poe using the Internet, produce original biographies, and author Poe-like narratives. Here is how Mike Wright explains what he does with the unit.

Comprehending Poe

To start the unit, we have students watch a film on the life and work of Edgar Alan Poe. Next, they silently read chosen short stories and poems by Poe. After that, I read the same selections orally as they follow along. I usually do one story a day. After each story we discuss the characters, theme, mood, the plot, the setting. Usually we focus on the similarities of Poe's stories. One of the things that comes out during the discussion of each story is the differences in the way they comprehended scenes when they read silently as compared to when they followed along as I read. Their silent reading, my oral reading, and the discussions improve comprehension greatly.

    After we finish several stories I bring a portable computer lab to class and the students use the Internet to find out things, print things, look at pictures, and, in general, browse the myriad sites about Poe. At this point we discuss what we have found by comparing and contrasting facts. There are differing facts about Poe's life and we try to identify "authentic" information compared to what seems to be opinion, speculation, or errors. We notice especially the differences between the film and any other facts they noticed on the Internet that might have been different. These include conflicting dates, the depth of his drug habits and alcoholism, and some mysteries about Poe's grave in Baltimore. A good site for this is http://www.poecentral.com/ This site has multiple sections including Poe's death and grave, a chronology of his life, where he lived, criticisms of his poems and stories, and information on his fiancée, Sarah Whitman.

Students take notes and I instruct and help them organize an outline for an essay about Poe. The first part is a biographical sketch based on the film and Internet research. The other part is a discussion of characteristics of Poe's writing, particularly the commonalties found in his stories. The students write a rough draft, go through the editing process, write final drafts, and submit the paper. The standard essay format of paragraphs with main ideas and supporting details is followed.

One of the teaching ideas I firmly believe in is that a writing teacher should be a model of someone who has mastered writing. I do this by writing the same essays I ask of the students.

Writing Like Poe

As a culminating activity, I read a half-finished short story that I have written in the style of Poe, but I leave it unresolved and open-ended. Students have to finish the story in the "style" of Poe based on their depth of knowledge of his writing. Here is the unfinished story:

> The night brought a wild storm, and the storm seemed to bring bad luck. I was driving in the deep countryside, returning from an exhausting trip to the city. The vast darkness of the sky and my unfamiliarity with the area put me in a confused state and soon I was wandering quite lost. So lost I was that even though my better judgment told me to beware, when I came upon the huge old house that stood ominously in the middle of that gigantic darkness, I realized I must take the opportunity and and try to get directions out of this maze.
>
> As I walked up the flagstone walk toward the house, the flashing of the lightning revealed a huge oaken door which had the head of a gargoyle as a knocker. Nervous, very nervous (in fact, my nerves jangle just to recall it) I knocked on the door of this seemingly demonic house.
>
> A man whom I assumed was the butler opened the door and beckoned me to enter. He was very tall and gaunt with grey, sunken cheeks and eyes, and was dressed entirely in black, and he moved in slow precise motions. He was pale and excepting that he was standing upright I would have believed him to be a cadaver. He remained silent as I explained my dilemma.

His steady corpse-like gaze made me feel edgy and uneasy, and a sickenly sweet odor from the house itself made me feel slightly ill. Wordlessly, he led me through a dark hallway into a chamber which seemed to be a library.

The smell, which swirled around me stronger now, a scent that seemed a combination of incense and old dusty furniture, was so overpowering that I felt as if I might faint.

My dreary escort left me in silence, and I stood feeling light-headed and anxious. A solitary candle, dripping wax, was burning on the table in the middle of the room and was the only source of illumination. As I said, the air was very heavy and the silence so complete that a terrible dread gripped my soul. In the eerie light, I noticed that one side of the room was lined with mirrors that were concave and completely distorted any image reflected in them. The other walls were hung in heavy crimson curtains from ceiling to floor.

At this point the students are to complete the story. Like all writing assignments, I give the requirements such as the number of words, some format tips, and then they write. Here is an example of a narrative written in Poe's style by an eighth-grade student.

The Haunted House

As I looked around so carefully, I noticed that this was not a library but merely a ballroom filled with covered furniture. Then I heard a thump, thump, thump. It sounded as if something were dragged and occasionally dropped. Now I was filled with such terror that my eyes grew wide and meticulous.

My eyes might have deceived me but I am sure that I saw a white figure standing on the other side of this room. Then music softly started to play and now I was very scared yes very scared that I ran swiftly away toward the exit. But all of a sudden my feet lost all contact with the ground and my face hit a concrete ground almost killing me. As I looked up I noticed a hole to the ballroom perhaps and figured I had fell in a deep dark hole. The odor was of a decaying body and the light in this contained are was almost nonexistent. It was very moist in the area that I saw little puddles everywhere. Then out from the ground came two straps strapping me down to the ground. I saw little white figures that brushed against my face. And when they did this my sweat froze and shattered into one million pieces.

After this I fell into a dreamless deep sleep. I had a nightmare of being killed on a sacrificial stone where my blood leaked from my body into drains and poured out. Then I heard a scream and woke up to notice there was a glass of water and crumbs of a loaf of bread beside me.

Then a marching row of fire ants came upon my vision. They came closer and closer to my waist where there was a strap restraining me to the hard icy floor. They covered the belt that I could not see it any longer. Then after they had left I noticed that the belt was eaten away. As I broke through the last strap I noticed the straps were made of sugar. Then I tried to climb to the top of the hole but I heard a grumbling sound from behind me. I saw a doll holding a piece of a mirror. As I climbed frantically to the top of the hole the doll chased right behind me. I reached the top and jumped out. I ran as fast as I could still dazed from what happened that I could not find a way out. I saw the doll climb slowly out of the hole. I was like a mouse in a trap doomed for life. The darkness ate my soul and as fear arose I was going crazy. I picked up a table and threw it at the screaming animal. It still came after me this time jumping on my leg stabbing it ten times as I fell to the ground. I kicked and tried to get back up but I couldn't. "Get off of me you crazy doll," I yelled.

Then the doll had disappeared. I slowly got back up and searched the area. Then I saw a door wide open but before that door were many of the same dolls. I was careful not to make a noise and watched as they were waiting for me either to try to escape or die. After two days of hunger I ran at the door full speed.

All the little creatures jumped on my body as I was eaten alive. The pain was enormous and I felt my hot blood touch what was left of my body. The dolls were satisfied and had left my suffering body. They only left my heart that kept pumping. It was if they wanted me to suffer more than I already had. A few seconds passed and I got dizzy.

"He he he," I heard from the little creatures.

"Help," I said. "Help me somebody," I said.

But there was no answer as I slowly died to the cold ground.

Summary

The examples in this chapter illustrate how language arts teachers structure lessons that enable students to use multiple sources, collect information, and produce a new text. The examples demonstrate how teachers provide formats, models, and examples that enable middle-grade students to conduct successful inquiry and communicate what they have learned to others.

Reference

Guy, C. L., & Wasserstein, P. (1996, Febuary 4). *The marriage of instruction and evaluation.* Paper presented at Colorado Council International Reading Association meeting in Denver.

10

Applied Literacy: Science in Middle School

Effective inquiry is more than just asking questions. A complex process is involved when individuals attempt to convert information and data into useful knowledge.

Joe Exline, 2001

This chapter features a detailed classroom example from a middle-school classroom in Marion, Illinois. Greg Reid uses a full-blown inquiry process to teach science. During the nine-week earth science unit featured here, the students do not follow a textbook with assignments and tests. Instead, they work in teams to compare and contrast organic and nonorganic farming. They test soil samples, study material on genetically modified organisms, conduct a consumer survey, and gather information and data from texts and the Internet. The problem they attempt to solve is whether or not a fictitious agribusiness, Heartland Produce, should switch from nonorganic to organic farming methods.

The Heartland Produce Project

Sitting in the back of the room I was struck by how the eighth-grade students entering Mr. Reid's classroom were all alike in one way—noisy and active. It didn't matter if they were sitting at their desks or standing in clumps of two or three—they were all moving their mouths and bodies in the ubiquitous adolescent between-class dance of middle school.

Organic or Nonorganic?

With the skill of a veteran middle-school teacher Greg easily quieted the students and directed the first group to gather around a laptop and a projector and start their PowerPoint presentation. Their recommendation was that Heartland Produce was to stay nonorganic and they presented twenty-two slides describing the evidence they had collected over the nine weeks. Their presentation featured a comparison of organic and nonorganic farming methods, information on genetically modified organisms, lab soil tests, and the results of a consumer survey on organic foods. The survey sampled parent and other adult views on organic food. Figure 10.1 shows five sample slides.

As I listened from the back of the room I noticed that, with the exception of one pair of students who passed notes on some out-of-class issue, the class was paying attention throughout the presentation and many questions were asked and answered. I also noticed that the group of presenters did not give a definite summary of reasons for their recommendation. Instead, we all had to infer that the data they presented led them to believe that nonorganic farming was easier, cheaper, the soil tests had mixed results that did not favor either organic or nonorganic, and the consumers they surveyed did not buy a lot of organic food.

During the presentation, Greg Reid did not interfere except to help with turn-taking when students asked questions of the panel. It was obvious the students were used to making these presentations and knew what to do. When the questioning ended, Greg called for the next group and they recommended that Heartland switch to organic farming. They had thirty-four slides of evidence. Figure 10.2 has five slides that illustrate their results and conclusion.

As this group finished, the class time was almost over, and Mr. Reid passed out evaluation sheets to all of the panel members who had presented during this class period. They completed one self-evaluation and a peer evaluation for each other member of their own work group.

Greg Reid says, "I put a lot of value on this peer evaluation process and so do the students; they seriously complete these rubric sheets." As an important aspect of cooperative learning, students learn that: effective work groups work together to achieve group goals, members get along well, members solve problems that arise, members perform different roles and tasks, and members encourage others and keep the group on-task. A copy of the self and group rubric is included in Appendix E.

In addition to the peer evaluations, Mr. Reid evaluates each group presentation using the following rubric.

Group Powerpoint Presentation Rubric

A. Slide show visual appearance/quality. Creates a slide show that
   4. exceeds conventional standards
   3. clearly meets conventional standards
   2. does not meet one or a few important standards
   1. does not address the majority of the conventional standards

As a group we have decided that Heartland Produce should not convert to Organic farming but stay with Nonorganic

Farming Organically

Organic Methods
- Organic farmers maintain their fertility by adding compost/manure.
- Organic farmers control pests by the "good bug" "bad bug" system which is adding beneficial insects such as spiders to eat the non-beneficial insects.

Nonorganic Methods
- Instead of waiting for cows to produce manure it is easier and less time consuming to just spray synthetic fertilizers.
- Instead of using the bugs it's more inexpensive to spray chemicals.

Farming Organically (cont.)

- Organic farmers use a method of spreading organic matter to smother the weeds.
- Organic farmers can't use GMO's.

- Nonorganic farmers use herbicides-much easier and cheaper and less time consuming.
- Nonorganic farmers can use GMO's to develop a resistant gene.

Soil Texture Lab

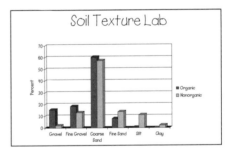

Buying Habits/Public Opinion

- Nobody buys the food except a certain few
- Even if people do buy the food-they only spend a tiny bit of their food bill on it

- More people don't know about organic food than do
- They said it was too expensive or they didn't care
- Some people even said it tasted bad

FIGURE 10.1

We recommend that Heartland Produce should switch to farming organically. In the following report we will include the following to support our recommendation and provide information about organic farming

Advantages of farming organically

Healthier for:

- Humans
  - No chemicals used so humans are less likely to be exposed to harmful particles

- Animals
  - Chemicals can't kill or hurt them

- Air
  - The air will be cleaner because of no chemicals or harmful pests in the air

- Water
  - Chemicals can't run off into the water supply and contaminate it

- Soil
  - No chemicals to kill off beneficial insects in the soil, which makes the soil healthier

GMOs
(Genetically Modified Organisms)

- A genetically modified organism is a bacterium, virus, or more complex life form whose DNA has been altered for a particular purpose.
- Organic farmers don't use GMOs.

Disadvantages of GMOs

- People might have allergic reactions
- Public reaction to the use of recombinant DNA when something has been genetically altered or mixed
- Environmentalists fear genetically modified plants may cross-breed with weeds. This would produce a weed that is resistant to some herbicides.

FIGURE 10.2

B. Accurately sorts information onto the correct slides
   4. correctly sorts every piece of information presented onto the correct slide. Slide contains information that is consistent with the title of the slide
   3. correctly sorts the majority of information onto the correct slide. One slide contains information that is not consistent with the title of the slide
   2. makes 2–3 errors in placing information onto the correct slide
   1. makes more than 4 errors in placing information onto the correct slide
C. Thoroughness. The presentation:
   4. covers all areas of research and shows a thorough understanding of all areas
   3. is missing one area of research or does not show a thorough understanding of 1–3 areas of research
   2. is missing 2–3 areas of research or does not show a thorough understanding of 4–6 research areas
   1. is missing over 4 areas of research or does not show a thorough understanding of any area of research
D. Spelling errors
   4. no spelling errors
   3. 1 spelling error
   2. 2–3 spelling errors
   1. many spelling errors
E. Group preparedness for presentation
   4. very well prepared for presentation
   3. well prepared for presentation
   2. less than well prepared for presentation
   1. not prepared at all for the presentation; very disorganized

The slide presentations and the student and teacher evaluations were the culmination of eight weeks of inquiry. Needless to say, I was impressed and I wondered what the teacher and students had done during that time that enabled them to present the data and their recommendations. The following section describes some of the science and applied literacy activities that led up to the Power-Point presentations.

Blazing Trails Science

Reid is part of the Illinois Blazing Trails consortium of teachers who are advocates for problem-based and inquiry-based learning in science. Blazing Trails is a grant-supported effort to improve science teaching in Illinois, and Reid is involved through his own teaching and by leading staff development sessions in which other teachers learn how to teach using problem-based learning and inquiry science lessons.

Reid introduces the unit with the following letter from the CEO of Heartland Produce. The letter assumes that the students are researchers who will investigate the pros and cons of switching from nonorganic to organic farming and make an informed recommendation.

Heartland Produce

• *Food production for the health of our customers and the environment* •

To: Heartland Research Team   September 1, 2000
From: Odo Coileus, CEO Heartland Produce
Subject: Conversion from a conventional farm to an organic farm

Research Team,

Since the early 1990s, the interest in organic gardening and the sale of organic produce has experienced an increase of public support. The organic produce and products market is currently a 6 billion dollars-per-year industry. Furthermore, due to the new National Organic Certification Standards, we believe that the sale of organic produce and products will increase dramatically over the next few years.

Organic production of produce is considered an environmentally safe way of producing fruits and vegetables and is considered by many to be more nutritious and healthier than nonorganic produce.

Due to the increased public demand for organic produce, Heartland Produce is considering converting our conventional vegetable farms to organic farms. Heartland would like to adopt an environmentally friendly approach to food production. We believe that by increasing the bio-diversity of our farms and by not using synthetic insecticides/pesticides, herbicides, and fungicides, we will help the environment, make our farm a healthier place for our workers, and produce a healthier product for our customers. However, we at Heartland have no experience in organic food production, have no data concerning the public's opinions or buying habits regarding organic versus nonorganic food, and have no data or information to support our personal beliefs. Additionally, we are concerned that, without using synthetic fertilizers to supply nutrients to the plants, the fertility of the soil, as well as the overall quality of the soil, will decrease over time. Furthermore, we are worried that without synthetic insecticides, pesticides, herbicides, and fungicides, our crop yields will be drastically lowered by damage caused by insects, fungi, and molds, and that the crops will be overrun by weeds. Moreover, with the new developments in genetic engineering and genetically modified organisms (GMOs), we need information concerning genetically modified organisms (specifically genetically modified crops) as well as the public's opinion and knowledge concerning GMOs. This information will be helpful if we decide not to go organic.

Heartland Produce is a business. As with any business we will not adopt any policy or procedure that does not make good business sense. We, as well as our stockholders, want to make a profit. We are, however, truly concerned about the welfare of the environment and the health of our workers and customers.

As a member of a research team hired by Heartland Produce, your job will be to make a professional PowerPoint presentation that will include a recommendation supported by scientific data, research, and reliable sources as to whether or not we should convert our farms to organic production. A full written report containing data and research supporting your recommendation will also be required. Additionally, all areas of concern and any questions raised throughout this letter need to be covered during your PowerPoint presentation and included in the written report. Your final recommendation and report will be presented to the Heartland Produce board members in approximately 9 weeks.

Good Luck,

Odo Coileus, CEO Heartland Produce

The letter is part of a packet of materials that contain the directions, formats, and the research learning activities the students will be involved in over the next nine weeks. Because it would take an entire book to show you all of the materials that Reid's students use, I have selected lessons and formats that illustrate how his students act as researchers and use their literacy skills in a science setting. The following document from the packet is for students and parents. It provides a clearer picture of what Reid expects students to accomplish as researchers.

Heartland Problem Statement

Role
How can we as members of a research team hired by Heartland Produce—

Task
Present a professional presentation to the members of the Heartland Produce board members—

Criteria
In such a way as to recommend whether Heartland should or should not convert their conventional vegetable farm to an organic vegetable farm?

A professional presentation will include:

1. PowerPoint presentation presented orally
2. written report to be turned in at the end of the PowerPoint presentation

3. posters (optional)
4. graphs
5. charts

Final Report/Recommendation needs to include:

1. clearly stated position on whether Heartland Produce should or should not convert their conventional vegetable farm to an organic vegetable farm
2. scientific data gathered from experiments and surveys supporting your argument
3. research supported by reliable sources supporting your argument

Include in your final report/recommendation thorough explanations of the following:

1. How does one grow food organically?
2. How does organic farming affect soil fertility (macronutrients and micronutrients)?
3. How does organic farming affect the overall quality of the soil's texture? pH? water holding capacity? organic matter? insect population? vertebrate/invertebrate population? bacteria population? etc.
4. How will increasing the bio-diversity of Heartland farm hurt or help the environment (plants, animals, insects, air, water, soil)?
5. By farming organically, how will Heartland be producing healthier food for their customers? (for example: more nutrient rich, no chemical residue, etc.)
6. Does Heartland's current use of synthetic insecticides/pesticides, herbicides, or fungicides affect their employee's health?
7. How does Heartland's current use of synthetic insecticides/pesticides, herbicides, or fungicides affect the environment (plants, animals, insects, air, water, soil)?
8. Can crop damage from insects be effectively controlled using organic measures vs. chemical measures?
9. Can crop damage from fungi and molds be effectively controlled using organic measures vs. chemical measures?
10. Can crop damage from weeds be effectively controlled using organic vs. chemical measures?
11. What is the difference in overall crop yield using organic vs. chemical measures?
12. If crop yield decreases, how might profit remain the same? Can Heartland make a profit if they convert to organic food production?
13. What is local public knowledge and opinion concerning organic food?
14. What are the local consumer's buying habits concerning organic food versus nonorganic food?

15. What are GMOs? What are the negatives and positives of GMOs?
16. How does the public perceive GMOs? Are they informed? Misinformed? Concerned? Apathetic?

Parents also receive the following letter that describes the kind of schoolwork the students will be involved in for next grading period.

Parents,

For several more weeks we will be working on the Heartland Produce project. This project is a Problem-Based Learning (PBL) activity, a teaching method that emphasizes guiding students to develop critical thinking and problem-solving skills that they may apply to real-world situations throughout their lifetimes. As with all PBL activities, the Heartland problem is ill-structured. By "ill-structured" I mean the project does not proceed in a linear fashion with predefined activities that are to be done in a specific order on a specific day, i.e., we will not be on Chapter 4, pages 5–10, on Monday and then pages 11–15 on Tuesday, etc. The activities done in class are student-generated, with the teacher acting as a facilitator of learning as opposed to the holder of information. Because of this, one class period's activities may differ from those of another class period. This is the general rule, as opposed to the exception, with PBL activities. For example, one class may decide to do an activity that requires an experiment, another class may be conducting research on the Internet, while another may be in the classroom developing and/or discussing a completely new activity that no other period is doing. Although all periods are engaged in different learning activities, they all are working toward a common goal: the solving of the problem presented to them by the "board members of Heartland Produce." Eight areas/questions that need to be covered for the Heartland Produce problem have been identified and pulled from the letter the students received from "the board members" of Heartland Produce. As stated above, it is possible that not all class periods will be investigating the same area/question at the same time or in the same manner. You will be informed about information, topics, and activities that each period has decided to cover, and the due dates for any papers, lab reports, or homework.

Sincerely,

Mr. Reid

As Reid states in the letter, in order to help students focus their inquiry, he has them gather data that answer eight key questions.

Key Questions: Heartland Produce Project

1. Will increasing the bio-diversity of the farm and not using synthetic insecticides/pesticides, herbicides, and fungicides:
   a. help the environment?
   b. make the farm a healthier place for their workers?
   c. allow Heartland to produce healthier food?
2. How do you farm organically?
3. What are some public opinions and buying habits regarding organic versus nonorganic food?
4. By not using synthetic fertilizers to supply nutrients to the plants, will the soil fertility and overall soil quality decrease?
5. By not using synthetic pesticides/insecticides, herbicides, and fungicides, will crop yields be drastically lowered due to damage caused by insects, fungi/molds, and weeds?
6. What information does Heartland need concerning GMOs?
7. What information information concerning the public's opinion and knowledge concerning GMOs does Heartland need?
8. If Heartland converts to organic, will they be able to make a profit?

Information Sources: Heartland Project

Information sources for this project include primary source evidence from science laboratory experiments and surveys that the students carry out. Secondary classroom and library text sources are also used. Reid provides lists of Web sites and students have access to the Internet in the school library located across the hallway from his classroom.

A Sample of Reid's Inquiry Activities

It would take an entire book to show you all of the materials and activities that Reid has arranged for this science unit. To illustrate what students do in his class, I've reproduced the following survey that students use to answer question three about consumer attitudes toward organic food.

Question Three

What are some public opinions and buying habits regarding organic versus nonorganic food?

Assignment: Consumer Survey on Organic Food

Directions: This survey is done after students have written their paper concerning the production of organic food, genetically modified organisms (GMO's), and the safety and health of food. It is best if the survey is one of the last things done during the Heartland project because only near the end of the project do students have enough broad knowledge to generate their own questions for the survey. Additionally, they will have the knowledge base to cover all important areas concerning organic food thoroughly.

Activities: Students will work in small groups and brainstorm possible survey questions and then, as a whole class, decide which questions to use on the survey form. Students will conduct the survey, and all the information will be compiled during a class period. Each group will analyze the data and come to its own conclusions. A sample of a student-developed survey follows.

Survey on Organic and Nonorganic Food

Please complete the following survey concerning organic vs. nonorganic food.

Age:
    12–18   _____
    19–25   _____
    26–50   _____
    over 51   _____

Sex: M _____   F _____

Income (optional):
    0–$30,000   _____
    $31,000–$50,000   _____
    $51,000–$100,000   _____
    over $100,000   _____

Education: Mark the highest education level you have attained.
    In Junior High or High School   _____
    High School diploma   _____
    2yr college degree   _____
    4yr college degree   _____
    Master's Degree   _____
    Doctorate   _____

1. Do you know what organic food is?   Y _____   N _____
2. Do you buy organic food?   Y _____   N _____
   If you answered no, go to question #3. If you answered yes, go to questions #4 and #5.

3. If you don't buy organic food, why don't you?
   a. It's too expensive _____
   b. It tastes bad _____
   c. Don't care if it's organic or not _____
   d. Don't know the difference between organic and nonorganic food _____
4. Why do you buy organic food? (Mark all that apply)
   a. It tastes better _____
   b. It is better for the environment _____
   c. It is chemical free _____
   d. It is more nutritious _____
   e. Other (explain) _____
5. What percentage of your food bill is spent on organic food?
   a. 1%– 25% _____
   b. 25%– 50% _____
   c. 50%– 75% _____
   d. 75%–100% _____

Thank you for your cooperation!

Results: See slides in Figure 10.1. Based on their own survey, the students found that organic food is only bought by a few people who spend a small portion of their food budget on organic food, most people don't know about organic food, and some said it was too expensive and tasted bad.

Comments and Observations on the Heartland Project

The teaching artifacts you have just viewed represent only a few of the materials needed for this science unit. As for as a time line, you will recall that, in the letter to parents, Reid said that the unit is not organized in a linear fashion so that all students move together from topic to topic. Instead, different students and different sections may be investigating the major questions at different times, using different sources and learning activities.

I talked to some students and parents about Reid's classes. Some believe the inquiry method is too open-ended and difficult, while others rave about how motivated the students are, how well they do, and how much they learn. I asked Reid about this and he told me that most students do fairly well, some do outstanding work, and a few do not do the assignments. He said that some students read the letter from the Heartland Produce CEO and immediately have a sense of how the various labs, surveys, and research activities will work. They usually earn grades of A and B. Others get the idea after they start working in teams and earn Bs and Cs. A few do not and at report card time they receive Ds and Fs.

This description of Reid's science classroom reveals how he is attempting to create a research environment. Reid believes in and trusts his students to work with the scientific method. He has been teaching middle-school science as serious inquiry long enough to know that, if he provides the materials and guidance, most, but not all, of his students will experience science directly from the inside. He is comfortable knowing that, in this environment, some students thrive and most survive. As for those who fail, Reid shows them and their parents the activities they decided not to do.

Summary

This example of inquiry in middle-grade science illustrates how students are engaged in authentic science inquiry from the inside. In order to learn soil science concepts, students act as researchers, create their own data to answer questions, and communicate their findings in a real-world context. The process is complex, detailed, and requires many teaching materials and formats that enable students to produce new information. In this example, the school is transformed into a working laboratory where apprentice scientists are guided by a master science teacher.

References

Exline, J. (2001). What is inquiry-based learning? On-line. Available at: www.wnet.org/wnetschool/concept2class/month6/index.html

Reid, G. (2000). *The Heartland Produce Project*. Unpublished classroom materials. Marion Junior High School, Marion, IL.

11

Final Words

In 2001 the seventh-grade students in James Berezow's and Michael Wright's social studies and language arts classes visited Native American archeological sites in Southern Illinois, photographed the pictographs and petroglyphs, and wrote interpretive captions. They also researched over fifteen different tribes that had lived in the region at one time or another. Teams of students took the pictures, captions, and information on the tribes and produced a Web site that tells about the Native American people who had once inhabited the hills and valleys in Southern Illinois. When you visit these seventh-grade classrooms, you see the students' large color photographs of the petroglyphs with informative captions displayed professionally on the walls. The display looks like a state or national museum of natural history and the Web site reads like a professional source. The level of communication is very impressive, especially when we know that seventh-grade students are the authors and publishers.

This book is purposely loaded with vignettes and stories like the above because I wanted to portray the many different ways that middle-grade students satisfy their curiosity. The result is a patchwork quilt-like book with many textures and patterns that may appear a bit messy. That's fine with me, because authentic inquiry is an active construction process that reflects how middle-grade children and teachers operate when they are consumed by curiosity.

At the heart of this curiosity and messiness are teachers who value children's questions and their boundless energy to wonder and know more. Instead of being put off by their pupils' energized activity, the teachers featured in this book (and many others I've yet to know) can harness the passion with authentic inquiry.

In my value system, the highest level of work in education is day in and day out classroom teaching that is engaging and satisfying to students. This book is a testament to teachers who relish the messiness, the noise, the wonder, and the sheer exuberance of middle graders who are chasing after a question or trying to resolve an issue. In many ways these teachers act like tour guides. They listen to their students to find out what the children already know, and they help to arrange a tour of new territory that the children are curious about. They are not afraid to let the children explore and they are ready to help the children when they encounter delays and detours.

At the heart of applied literacy is my firm belief that children are not empty of knowledge, they are full of wonder. In the middle grades they have an incredible capacity to have wonderful ideas that teachers use to fuel the learning process. The stories, the lessons, and the technical teaching ideas in this book provide a close look at what happens in classrooms when teachers help children use their literacy skills to explore, validate, and display these wonderful ideas.

Appendix A

Student Reading Rubric

Purpose

4 • By myself I choose and read many different kinds of books.
  • Without help I find and use the references I need to answer my questions.
  • I change the speed of my reading depending on what I am reading.

3 • I read many different kinds of books.
  • When references are provided, I use them to answer my questions.
  • I remind myself to change the speed of my reading depending on what I am reading.

2 • With my teacher's help, I read different kinds of books.
  • With my teacher's help, I use references to answer my questions.
  • When my teacher reminds me, I change the speed of my reading.

1 • I read books I know.
  • It is difficult for me to use references.
  • I always read at the same rate.

Technical Strategies

4 • I automatically use written conventions (punctuation and capitalization) to understand what I am reading.
  • I use a variety of resources and strategies to understand new words.
  • I use letter sounds and word parts to figure out complex words.
  • I add words that I learned into my personal working vocabulary.
  • I use the way letters and parts of words are put together to help me read and understand words.

3 • I think about written conventions to understand what I am reading.
  • I use the words and ideas in the sentence to help me read and understand a word I do not know, and I may use the dictionary.
  • I use letter sounds and word parts to sound out words.

- I add words that I learned to my reading and listening vocabulary.
- I am beginning to look at the way letters and parts of words are put together to help me read words.

2 • I am beginning to recognize that written conventions can help me understand what I am reading.
- I use picture clues and other words and ideas in my reading to read a word I do not know.
- I use letter sounds to figure out some words.
- I read words that I have seen before.
- I am beginning to see that words have letters and parts that are the same.

1 • I read one word at a time. I am not using conventions to help me understand what I am reading.
- I recognize and read words that I see every day in my community (street signs, store names, etc.).
- I know all the letters and most of my sounds.
- I understand that groups of letters make words and have meaning.
- I read simple words.

Comprehension/Interpretation Strategies

4 • To help me understand what I read, I read between the lines, predict what will happen, ask myself questions, question what the author was thinking, and form creative or unusual ideas about what I read. By looking at the parts of the text, I better understand the content. I make unique connections that I can defend.
- I know what to do when I do not understand. I question and review. If I need to, I change my thinking.
- I clearly and briefly summarize the main idea.
- I describe or draw detailed pictures from my mind that help me understand what I have read.

3 • To help me understand what I read, I describe what I read, predict what will happen, ask myself questions and form my own ideas about what I read. I identify and describe the parts of the text. I make some connections that I can defend.
- I usually know what to do when I do not understand. I sometimes question and review what I read, and, if I need to, change my thinking.
- I summarize the main idea.
- I describe or draw pictures from my mind that helps me understand what I have read.

2 • To help me understand what I read, I remember what I have read and begin to predict what will happen.
   • I am not always sure what to do when I do not understand. I sometimes ask for help.
   • I retell what I have read.
   • I describe or draw simple pictures from my mind that help me understand what I have read. My pictures may need more details.

1 • It is hard for me to understand what I read.
   • I need to learn what to do when I am having trouble.
   • I retell some of what I have read.
   • I sometimes use the author's pictures to help me understand what I have read.

Background Knowledge

4 • My rich vocabulary and extensive knowledge of my world help me compare what I am reading to what I already know. I predict what will happen using the words and the pictures.

3 • I predict what will happen or draw conclusions using what I already know, good vocabulary, the text, and the pictures.

2 • With help, I use things I already know, limited vocabulary, the text, and the pictures to understand what I am reading.

1 • I do not show that I already know important things about the topic. With help, I use the text and pictures to understand what I am reading.

Student Writing Rubric

Ideas and Content

4 • My writing skillfully meets the requirements of the task and is interesting to the reader.
   • I show that I know my topic well and express ideas that are interesting and unique. I write thoughtfully about my ideas and weave them together to improve meaning.
   • I stick to my topic and clearly communicate important ideas, carefully choosing details that make my subject clear and interesting.

3 • My writing meets the requirements of the task and is interesting to the reader.
   • I show that I know my topic well and communicate my ideas to the reader.

- I stick to my topic. I have enough details to make the topic clear and keep the reader interested.

2 • My writing makes sense, but I did not meet all of the requirements of the task.
   • I know my topic, but I need to include more information in my writing.
   • I may have spent too much time on information that was not important or not enough time on important ideas.

1 • My main idea was not clear, and I did not meet the requirements of the task.
   • I need more information about my topic.
   • I did not stick to my topic, or I did not have much to say.

Organization

4 • I plan the order of my writing according to the purpose and my ideas move smoothly from one to another. I place details to strengthen my ideas.
   • I write a unique beginning and ending that make my writing memorable.
   • I carefully weave the details into my writing to make my ideas clear to the reader.

3 • I think about and organize my writing to fit the purpose. My details are in the right place.
   • I have an interesting beginning that gets the reader's attention. My ending leaves the reader satisfied.
   • My ideas are connected.

2 • I need to give more thought to organization to meet the purpose of my writing. Some details may be misplaced or unimportant, making my writing confusing to the reader.
   • I have a beginning and end but one or both may be weak.
   • Some of my ideas are connected, but my transitions are not smooth.

1 • My organization is confusing and does not fit the purpose.
   • My writing does not have a beginning or end, or I may need to improve them.
   • The order of my paper is confusing. My ideas are not connected. My transitions are weak or missing.

Voice

4 • I have written in a way that shows the reader how I really think and feel. My writing sounds distinctly like me.

- I choose words that sincerely and strongly express my ideas in a personal way.
- When people read my writing, they will be informed, challenged, amused, surprised, delighted, or moved.
- My audience clearly understands my purpose.

3 • I have put something of myself into my writing, and the reader can recognize my voice.
- I put words together that naturally express my ideas.
- I hold the interest of my audience with my expressive writing.
- I am aware of my audience and the purpose for writing.

2 • Most of my writing sounds like me and not someone else.
- My words are expressed in an ordinary way.
- I sometimes address my audience and the purpose for my writing.

1 • My writing can be understood, but I need to show my feelings.
- I have not used my writer's voice.
- I do not speak to my audience or to the purpose when I write.

Word Choice

4 • I carefully choose words that help me show a thorough understanding of my topic.
- I use a variety of action and descriptive words to make my writing exciting. I use unexpected or unusual words appropriately.

3 • I accurately choose the words I need that show an understanding of my topic.
- I use a variety of action and descriptive words to make my writing interesting.

2 • Some of my words fit my writing, but some do not show that I understand my topic.
- My audience understands my message, but I need to find words that are interesting.

1 • I do not use the right words to say what I meant.
- I use the same words over and over.

Sentence Structure

4 • My sentences are well formed. I use different kinds of sentences. My sentences clearly express my thoughts.
- I purposely made some sentences longer than others did, and they do not all begin in the same way.

- My sentences are well formed, focused on the topic, and have few unneeded words.
- Dialogue (when used) makes my writing more interesting, and it sounds like real people talking.

3 • Most of my sentences are well formed and express my thoughts.
- My sentences focus on the topic. I rarely use unneeded words.
- Dialogue (when used) usually sounds like real people talking.

2 • My sentence formation makes my writing difficult to understand.
- My sentences need to focus on the topic.
- My sentences are too short or too long.
- I need help writing dialogue.

1 • My sentences are hard to read and understand.

Writing Conventions

4 • My writing has few, if any, errors in spelling, punctuation, capitalization, and grammar. I use paragraphs correctly.

3 • My punctuation, spelling, and grammar are usually correct. If I make errors, they do not interfere with meaning. I use paragraphs correctly for the beginning, middle, and end.

2 • My end punctuation us usually correct. I may need help with other punctuation. I spell familiar words correctly. I need help correcting grammar. I need help knowing how to use paragraphs in my writing.

1 • My writing has many errors in spelling, punctuation, and grammar. I am not yet writing in paragraphs.

Student Speaking Rubric

Ideas and Content

4 • I communicate to the audience the purpose of my speech (to inform, explain, demonstrate, entertain, or persuade), and I keep my audience's attention and interest throughout the whole speech.
- My speech proves that I know my topic very well.
- I can take the information I have learned about my topic, understand it, and communicate it to my audience in my own words. (interpret)
- I communicate important ideas. Each idea fits into the whole speech. My speech includes the details necessary to make my topic clear and interesting. (analyze)

- I thoughtfully and carefully choose vocabulary that shows a thorough understanding of my topic.

3 • I communicate to the audience the purpose of my speech (to inform, explain, demonstrate, entertain, or persuade) and keep my audience's attention and interest most of the time.
- My speech proves that I know my topic.
- I stay focused on my topic.
- I communicate important ideas.
- I include some details that support the main ideas.
- I choose vocabulary that shows I understand my topic.

2 • My audience may understand the purpose of my speech but I may not have included all the necessary parts.
- Some of my ideas are clear. Some may not fit with the main idea.
- I may spend too much or not enough time on certain details.
- I use ordinary or confusing words.

1 • My audience does not understand my purpose.
- I do not know my topic or I do not stay on my topic.
- I use simple words and may repeat the same words or use confusing words.

Organization

4 • My speech is well organized and I place details in a way that helps my audience clearly understand my purpose (to inform, explain, demonstrate, entertain, or persuade).
- I include a unique and powerful beginning that draws the audience in and my conclusion strongly impacts my audience.
- The ideas in my speech are in the correct and logical order and naturally flow from one part to the next.

3 • My speech is organized and the details support the purpose.
- I include an inviting beginning that draws the audience in and my conclusion lets my audience know my speech is ending.
- My ideas are in the correct order but some of my ideas do not flow naturally from one part to the next. I may overuse words like *then* or *and*.

2 • My speech shows some organization but the audience may not understand the purpose or may sometimes be confused.
- I have a beginning, middle, and end, but they may be too brief.
- I may have a hard time moving from one part to the next in my speech.

1 • My speech is not well organized. My main ideas are not clear.
- I may be missing a beginning, middle, or end.
- My ideas are not in a logical order.

Voice

4 • My voice is loud enough and clear enough to keep my audience's interest and attention for the whole speech.
  • I watch my audience to see if I need to speak faster or slower to make my speech more interesting or easier to understand.
  • I use appropriate expression to make my ideas clear. I am able to either amuse, surprise, challenge, delight, or move the audience throughout my speech.
  • I have a unique style of speaking that enables me to express my personality in my speech.

3 • My voice is loud and clear enough for the audience to understand.
  • The rate of my speech is appropriate.
  • I use expression in my speech. I sometimes either amuse, surprise, challenge, delight, or move the audience.
  • I use style and personality to express myself.

2 • My voice is loud and clear enough for the people close to me to hear.
  • Sometimes I speak too fast or too slow.
  • Sometimes I use certain words that interfere with my message (for example, *um, you know, like*).
  • I use some expression or style in my speech.

1 • I do not speak loudly or clearly enough.
  • I speak too fast or too slow.
  • Often I use certain words that interfere with my message (for example, *um, you know, like*).
  • I do not use expression or style in my speech.

Student Listening Rubric

4 • I explain and understand the reason for listening, and I connect this information to new ideas and situations.
  • I ask thoughtful questions to help me gain more information. I review what I hear and apply it to other subjects and situations.
  • I make unexpected connections between what I hear and my own experiences.
  • I summarize the main idea and details to explain the speaker's message.

3 • I understand the reason for listening.
  • I review what I hear and ask questions to better understand the speaker's message.

- I make some unexpected connections between what I hear and my own experience.
- I am able to retell the main idea and details of the speaker's message.

2 • Sometimes I understand the reason for listening.
- With help, I answer both simple and difficult questions about what I hear.
- I make expected connections between what I hear and my experiences.
- I retell the main idea of the speaker's message.

1 • It is hard for me to understand the reason for listening.
- With help, I answer simple questions about what I hear.
- It is hard for me to make connections between what I hear and my experiences.
- It is hard for me to retell the main idea of the speaker's message.

These rubrics are based on the Colorado learning outcomes. When students used the rubrics they learned important critical thinking skills while they assessed and monitored changes in their own literacy performance. When teachers were asked to defend their teaching, they showed parents and the community portfolios of written products of the students. They also showed parents the accompanying rubric ratings that the students produced while they read, wrote, spoke, and listened to reports on birds of prey. Matching the state outcomes to teaching and learning with the rubrics went a long way to meet both the teachers' and the community's concerns for accountability.

Source: Guy, C. L., & Wasserstein, P. (1996, February 4). *The marriage of instruction and evaluation.* Paper presented at Colorado Council International Reading Association meeting in Denver.

Appendix B

IRA/NCTE Standards For
The English Language Arts

1. Students read a wide variety of print and nonprint texts to build an understanding of texts, of themselves, and of the cultures of the United States and the world; to acquire new information; to respond to the needs and demands of society and the workplace; and for personal fulfillment. Among these texts are fiction and nonfiction, classic and contemporary works.

2. Students read a wide range of literature from many periods in many genres to build an understanding of the many dimensions (e.g., philosophical, ethical, aesthetic) of human experience.

3. Students apply a wide range of strategies to comprehend, interpret, evaluate, and appreciate texts. They draw on their prior experience, their interactions with other readers and writers, their knowledge of word meanings and of other texts, their word identification strategies, and their understanding of textual features (e.g., sound–letter correspondence, sentence structure, context, graphics).

4. Students adjust their use of spoken, written, and visual language (e.g., conventions, style, vocabulary) to communicate effectively with a variety of audiences and for different purposes.

5. Students employ a wide range of strategies as they write and use different writing process elements appropriately to communicate with different audiences for a variety of purposes.

6. Students apply knowledge of language structure, language conventions (e.g., spelling and punctuation), media techniques, figurative language, and genre to create, critique, and discuss print and nonprint texts.

7. Students conduct research on issues and interests by generating ideas and questions, and by posing problems. They gather, evaluate, and synthesize data from a variety of sources (e.g., print and nonprint texts, artifacts, people) to communicate their discoveries in ways that suit their purpose and audience.

8. Students use a variety of technological and informational resources (e.g., libraries, databases, computer networks, video) to gather and synthesize information and to create and communicate knowledge.

9. Students develop an understanding of and respect for diversity in language use, patterns, and dialects across culture, ethnic groups, geographic regions, and social roles.

10. Students whose first language is not English make use of their first language to develop competency in the English language arts and to develop understanding of content across the curriculum.

11. Students participate as knowledgeable, reflective, creative, and critical members of a variety of literacy communities.

12. Students use spoken, written, and visual language to accomplish their own purposes (e.g., for learning, enjoyment, persuasion, and the exchange of information).

Source: Standards for the English Language Arts. (1996) Urbana, IL: National Council of Teachers of English, and Newark DE: International Reading Association (p. 25).

Appendix C

Tips For Using Search Engines

In addition to the mainstream search engines and the Web sites referred to in the text, there are search engines designed for student use. Some of the major ones that are designed for use by students include:

Kids Click!	http://www.kidsclick.org
Ask Jeeves for Kids	http://www.ajkids.com
Yahooligans!	http://www.yahooligans.com
Awesome Library	http://www.awesomelibrary.org

Some tips for students and teachers who are searching Web sites include (Kuntz, 2001):

Write down a word or phrase that describes the topic. Do not use abbreviations.

Think of a broader topic that might include the word or phrase. For example if the phrase is Battle of the Bulge look under World War II or U.S. History.

If the word is found then follow the path of subcategories to see if the target word is found under the broad category.

If categories do not work or if the search tool has no categories, try typing the word in the "search" box.

If nothing is found, check spelling. If the typed word had punctuation, try it without the punctuation.

If this doesn't work, try the five steps in another student search engine or go to a larger mainstream search engine like Google or Ask Jeeves.

At this point, if none of the methods work, students should ask for help from an adult. A parent, a teacher, a librarian can intervene at this point. Kuntz says elementary students should spend no more than ten minutes searching on their own before asking for help; older students can search for up to twenty minutes on their own.

Source: Kuntz, J. (2001, May). Teach and they shall find. *School Library Journal, 47*(5), 54–56.

Appendix D

Web Sites Mentioned in This Text

The following web sites were referred to in the text:

http://www.siec.k12.in.us/~west/online/index.html
This site has tutorials for creating Web sites which are especially well done.

http://www.marshall-es.marshall.k12.tn.us/jobe/
Hazel's Homepage includes a wide variety of interesting links including assistance for getting started on the Internet.

http://www.stemnet.nf.ca/CITE/themes.html
This site contains links to Internet sites that support thematic studies, so using it helps avoid random surfing. It also links students to "safe" sites that are appropriate for children.

http://www.nara.gov/exhall/exhibits.html
The National Archives Web site displays a multitude of interesting original historical documents.

http://www.media-awareness.ca/
This site contains a section called "Kid Power" that features true stories of kids who took a stand and spoke out. Teachers use it to motivate student writing and critical thinking.

http://members.aol.com/xxmindyxx/evaluate/intro.html

http://www.uwec.edu/Admin/Library/10cs.html

http://www.ala.org/parentspage/greatsites/criteria.html
These three sites are excellent resources for teachers and parents concerned about safe Web sites.

http://school.discovery.com/schrockguide/eval.html
> Kathy Shrock's site has excellent lessons and sets of questions that students can use to evaluate individual Web sites.

http://mciu.org/~spjvweb/evalwebteach.html
> Joyce Valenza's site has detailed lessons, sets of questions, and scoring rubrics for comparing different Web sites.

Favorite Web Sites Teachers Use

http://www.ala.org/ICONN/evaluate.html
> The American Association of School Librarians maintains this excellent site and it is the basic starting point for anyone evaluating Web sites.

http://www.cyberbee.com/guides.html
> Karen McLachlan has developed this site with guides teachers and students use to check the content and graphic design of home pages.

http://www.kn.pacbell.com/wired/bluewebn
> This site identifies Blue Ribbon Web sites and categorizes them by grade level, content area, and type of site. An evaluation rubric is used to assess all sites. Local schools can adapt the rubric.

http://www.acs.ucalgary.ca/~dkbrown
> The Children's Literature Web Guide is an excellent Internet resource that pulls all kinds of Internet sources that relate to books for Children and Young Adults.

http://www.askanexpert.com/
> This is an easy starter site that teachers use when they introduce children to the Web. Students can send a question and get an answer.

http://www.gsn.org/
> The Global Schoolhouse is an easy way for students to interact with other students by responding to surveys posted by other classes.

http://www.epals.com
> This site is called ePals where students find others to exchange E-mail with.

http://www.lightspan.com
> This site contains the Learning Search service with combined search results from different sources, specially selected sites for school, encyclopedia articles, teaching and learning activities, and lesson plans.

Appendix E

Peer and Team Evaluation for Heartland Project

A. Works toward the achievement of group goals.

    4. Actively helps identify group goals and works hard to meet them. Did more than enough research for the group, produced his or her fair share of slides for the group, and actively participated and wrote his or her fair share of the report without being told to do so.

    3. Communicates commitment to the group goals and effectively carries out assigned jobs. Carried out research for the group, produced his or her fair share of slides, and contributed his or her fair share to the report, but only after being told to do so because, if he or she did not, it would affect his or her grade.

    2. Communicates a commitment to the group goals but did not carry out assigned jobs such as doing his or her fair share of research, producing his or her fair share of slides for the group, or writing his or her fair share of the report. Did only a minimum amount of research, produced only the minimum amount of slides for the group, and contributed only the minimum amount to writing of the report.

    1. Does not work toward group goals or actively works against them. Did not do any research that helped the group, did not produce any slides for the group, or did not help with the writing of the report.

B. Demonstrates effective interpersonal skills. Got along well with other members of the group.

    4. Actively promotes effective group interaction and the expression of ideas and opinions in a way that is sensitive to the feelings and knowledge base of others. Did not make fun of anyone in the group and actively supported and helped other group members carry out his or her assigned jobs.

    3. Participates in group interaction without prompting. Expresses ideas and opinions in a way that is sensitive to the feelings and knowledge base of others. However, at times he or she was not sensitive to the feelings of other members in the group. Made fun of other members some of the time.

2. Participates in group interaction only after being prompted to do so. Expressed his or her ideas and opinions without considering the feelings and knowledge base of others. Made fun of other group members and only stopped after being told to do so.

1. Does not participate in group interaction, even after being told to do so. Was not sensitive to the feelings and knowledge base of others and constantly made fun of other group members.

C. Contributes to group maintenance. Helps the group identify what needs to be done in order for the group to complete the assignment.

  4. Actively helps the group identify what needs to be done in order to complete the assignment. This includes what research needs to be done, what slides need to be made, and what needs to be written for the report. He or she then actively, without being told to do so, carries out the research, makes slides, and begins writing the report.

  3. Helps the group identify what needs to be done in order to complete the assignment. This includes what research needs to be done, what slides need to be made, and what parts of the report need to be written. He or she then does research, makes slides and writes the report, only after being told to do so.

  2. Helps the group identify what needs to be done in order to complete the assignment only after being told to help out. He or she then does research, makes slides, and contributes to the writing of the report only after being told to do so.

  1. Does not attempt to identify what needs to be done in order to complete the assignment even when being told to do so. He or she refuses to carry out research, produce slides, or help write the report for the group.

D. Effectively performs a variety of roles within the group.

  4. Effectively performs multiple roles within the group. This includes identifying what research needs to be done and carrying out the research, identifying what slides need to be made and making the slides, identifying what order the slides need to be in, and identifying what needs to be included in the report, and then helping with the writing of the report.

  3. Effectively performs several but not all the roles required within the group.

  2. Makes an attempt to perform more only a few of the roles within the group but has little success doing so, such as not being able to find research information for the group, having trouble making PowerPoint slides, or writing the paper.

  1. Rejects opportunities or requests to perform more than one role in the group. Does not carry out research, the making of slides, or the writing of the report.

E. Makes sure that the group works well together.

    4. Encourages the group to evaluate how well they are working together. He or she tries to get everyone involved in thinking of ways to make changes when the group needs to improve. When the group decides to make changes, he or she makes sure the changes help the group to work better together.

    3. Participates in discussions of how well the group is working together and helps to develop suggestions for changes when the group needs to improve. He or she works on making the changes that the group agrees to.

    2. Participates in discussions of how well the group is working together only when he or she is asked to do so but does not have any ideas of his or her own for ways to change. When changes are decided, he or she puts little effort into making those changes.

    1. Does not participate in discussions of how well the group is working together and refuses to help work on the changes.

Index